# The Cross and the Crucifixion

Grace Dola Balogun

"Don't be alarmed," he said.
"You are looking for
Jesus the Nazarene,
who was crucified.
**He has risen!**
He is not here.
See the place where
they laid him."

Mark 16:6

# The Cross and the Crucifixion

Grace Dola Balogun

*Grace*
RELIGIOUS BOOKS
Publishing & Distributor

Grace Religious Books
New York, NY

The Cross and the Crucifixion
By Grace Dola Balogun
Copyright © 2012 Grace Dola Balogun
Cover design by Lionsgate Book Design, Lisa Hainline
   www.lionsgatebookdesign.com
Interior Design by White Cottage Publishing Company
   www.whitecottagepublishing.com

All rights reserved. No part of this book may be used or reproduced by any means, graphic, electronic, or mechanical, including photocopying, recording, taping, or by any information storage retrieval system without the written permission of the publisher except in the case of brief quotations embodied in critical articles and reviews.

Scripture quotations are from the Holy Bible, New International Version®, NIV®. Copyright © 1973, 1978, 1984 by International Bible Society. Used by permission of Zondervan. All rights reserved. (www.zondervan.com)

Grace Religious Books Publishing & Distributors books may be ordered through booksellers or by contacting the publisher:

Grace Religious Books Publishing & Distributors, Inc.
213 Bennett Avenue
New York, NY 10040
www.Gracereligiousbookspublishers.com
To contact the author: 1-646-559-2533
info@gracereligiousbookspublishers.com

ISBN: 978-0-9851980-3-9 (epub)
ISBN: 978-0-9851980-4-6 (pdf)
ISBN: 978-0-9851980-2-2 (sc)
Library of Congress Control Number: 2011960494
Printed in the United States of America

*I dedicate this book to our Lord and Savior Jesus Christ, the one and only, the crucified one, our Redeemer King. Through the Cross, He took my sins and my shame and the sins of everyone on earth upon Himself, so that we could be saved and receive the gift of grace and the incomparable inheritance from God the Father, as His adopted children: "See what great love the Father has lavished on us, that we should be called children of God! And that is what we are! The reason the world does not know us is that it did not know him." 1 John 3:1. He shed His precious blood on the Cross for my sins and the sins of the whole world. This book comes from Him and it is for Him, for His work of redemption, forever completed. I dedicate it to His glory now and forever.*

# Contents

| | |
|---|---|
| Preface | vii |
| 1. The Power of the Cross | 1 |
| 2. The Foreknowledge of God | 7 |
| 3. The First Adam and the Second Adam | 27 |
| 4. "Father Forgive Them; for They Do Not Know What They Are Doing." Luke 3:34 | 32 |
| 5. "Truly: I Tell You, Today You Will Be with Me in Paradise." Luke 23:43 | 39 |
| 6. "Woman, Here Is Your Son . . . Here Is Your Mother." John 19:26-27 | 45 |
| 7. "Eloi, Eloi, Lema Sabachthani? My God, My God, Why Have You Forsaken Me?" Mark 15:34 | 52 |
| 8. "I Am Thirsty." John. 19:28 | 57 |
| 9. "It Is Finished." John 19:30 | 66 |
| 10. "Father, Into Your Hands I Commit My Spirit." Luke 23:46 | 78 |
| 11. The Significance of the Number Seven from Creation | 95 |
| 12. The Meaning of the Cross as Found in God's Purpose | 109 |
| Excerpt from Elizabeth C. Clephane's 1872 Song | 120 |
| Summary | 123 |
| Final Word | 128 |
| Benediction | 133 |
| Biblical Index | 134 |
| About the Author | 139 |

# Preface

The title of this book is perhaps too comprehensive. Some readers might be expecting the dismissal of the Cross of Christ and Crucifixion. But it is on an orderly, full interpretation of the meaning and the power of the Cross the basis why Christ had to go to the Cross and be crucified in order to save sinners.

The people of God need a clearer explanation and more accurate clarification of the work of redemption. What Christ has done in the universe will not be repeated. He did it once and for all. Jesus' words and prayers in the garden of Gethsemane clearly show that the Father sent Him to the world for the remission of the sins of the human race: "My soul is overwhelmed with sorrow to the point of death." Mark 14:34.

Christ Jesus poured out the agony of His soul in prayer and submission to the Father's will. We can never know the intensity of Jesus' agonizing Spirit or the contents of the cup that He was going to drink, but he said: "Abba, Father . . . everything is possible for you. Take this cup from me. Yet not what I will, but what you will." Mark 14:36.

One thing of which we can be sure is that, when we go through our own suffering, in our own Gethsemane, Jesus Christ will be there with us, sympathizing and giving His own example of suffering and words of victorious submission: "Yet not what I will, but what you will."

This book has been put forward with the prayer that it may help many who need clear words of truth about the Cross and the crucifixion of Jesus Christ, the Son of God. It has been my desire to connect the work of redemption of Christ's suffering and agony on the Cross on the day of crucifixion to a clearer image of personal sacrifice on the part of Christ, our Lord.

Together we will be able to see Christ on the Cross on every page of this book. It is a journey in appreciating the redemptive power of the Cross to thank Him more than ever before in our lives.

Jesus Christ was the only one who had the power to forgive sin during His life on earth. He paid for our sins on the Cross with His precious blood and foretold that the Son of man had the power on earth to forgive sins: "But I want you to know that the Son of Man has authority on earth to forgive sins." So he said to the paralyzed man, "Get up, take your mat and go home." Matt 9:6.

Before He paid ransom for the sins of the whole world, Christ had the power to forgive sin on earth. He still forgives the sins of humanity today, and will continue until His return to the earth to judge as the book of Revelations tells us. Readers must know at the moment of reading this book that, however great their sin, Christ has the power and authority to forgive them, just as He did during His earthly ministry.

A touch from Him will leave you completely clean from your sins and the nature of sin. Jesus Christ's atoning work on the Cross has done just that. Christ has had unlimited power, since He conquered sin and since His resurrection from the dead, sitting at the right hand of God, interceding for us, and pleading our case before the Father. Christ's power to forgive sins still continues at the right hand of God.

He wants all of the people of this earth to repent and pray for forgiveness of their sins, which can only be achieved or obtained through Him. He is ready to forgive you for your sins today with blessed assurance. Christ will breathe on you the breath of life with the peace of God that surpasses all understanding—the peace of God that flows from the full forgiveness of all of your sins.

All people of this earth should believe in and experience the power of the Cross and crucifixion of Christ Jesus to forgive sin. Surrender all to the Savior, call on Him with a repentant heart, and you will receive forgiveness of your sins and a new life in Him.

"Jesus entered the temple courts, and, while he was teaching, the chief priests and the elders of the people came to him. 'By what authority are you doing these things?' they asked. 'And who gave you this authority?'" Matt 21:23.

Jesus had said to them earlier, during one of His sermons, "All things have been committed to me by my Father. No one knows the Son except the Father, and no one knows the Father except the Son and those to whom the Son chooses to reveal him." Matt 11:27.

And, after His resurrection, He told His Disciples: "Then Jesus came to them and said, 'All authority in heaven and on earth has been given to me'" Matt 28:18. All power is in Jesus' hands. We have to remember that the wind and waves of the sea obeyed and answered His command: "He got up, rebuked the wind and said to the waves, 'Quiet! Be still!' Then the wind died down and it was completely calm. " Mark 4:39.

Jesus Christ exercised His power on His creation during His earthly ministry. There should be no doubt in our minds that Christ is the only one who forgave sins on earth and, now, forgives sins in heaven because He lives forevermore.

# 1

# The Power of the Cross

There is no liberation or redemption that is as valuable, significant, or as glorious as the work of humanity from the beginning of creation of the world continues and ends in the Cross of Jesus Christ. Creation and the Crucifixion of Jesus Christ are inseparable. Its ongoing power is life transforming, and it works every second of every hour of the day.

> "*In addition to forgiveness, Jesus made us alive in Him, so that we could live victorious lives.*"

Many believers know that the Cross means their sins are forgiven. What some people need to realize is that, in addition to forgiveness, Jesus made us alive in Him, so that we could live victorious lives. His sacrifice has infused us with life, a brand new radiant energy.

## The Cross and the Crucifixion

The scripture tells us how many Christians have applied the finished work of Christ to their lives and have been transformed: "For we are to God the pleasing aroma of Christ among those who are being saved and those who are perishing. To the one we are an aroma that brings death; to the other, an aroma that brings life."Who is equal to such a task? Unlike so many, we do not peddle the word of God for profit. On the contrary, in Christ we speak before God with sincerity, as those sent from God." 2 Cor 2:15-17.

And, Apostle Paul said, "May I never boast except in the Cross of our Lord Jesus Christ, through which the world has been crucified to me, and I to the world." Gal 6:14. Those who glory, must glory, in the Cross of Christ. It was on the Cross that Christ defeated death.

> *"Jesus purchased all the glory, life, and freedom that we could ever contain. He died for us on the Cross and arose."*

And it was there that Jesus purchased all the glory, life, and freedom that we could ever contain. Jesus Christ paid the price for our sins, so we wouldn't have to die, because Christ died for us on the Cross and arose.

He defeated the power of sin and death in the lives of every person who believes in His Holy name. "For even the Son of Man did not come to be served, but to

## The Cross and the Crucifixion

serve, and to give his life as a ransom for many." Mark 10:45.

The seven last words of Christ on the Cross were spoken in the following order, from nine o'clock until noon: the Word of Forgiveness, "Jesus said, 'Father, forgive them, for they do not know what they are doing.' And they divided up his clothes by casting lots." Luke 23:34.

The Word of Salvation which was, "Jesus answered him, "Truly I tell you, today you will be with me in paradise." Luke 23:43.

The Word of Love, "Woman, here is your son," and to the disciple, "Here is your mother." John 19:26-27.

There were three hours of darkness, from noon until three o'clock, when no words were reported. Then, from three o'clock onward, He gave the Word of Spiritual Suffering, "'Eloi, Eloi, lema sabachthani?' (which means 'My God, my God, why have you forsaken me'?)" Mark 15:34.

Then, there was the Word of Physical Suffering: "I am thirsty." John 19:28.

Finally, came the Word of Triumph: "It is finished." John 19:30; and, the Word of Committal: "Father, into your hands I commit my spirit." Luke 23:46.

At each painful word Christ uttered, there were witnesses to hear his words and see his pain. The human heart is full of darkness towards its fellow man.

## The Cross and the Crucifixion

The people of those days were the same as the people of today. They took pleasure in violence.

This shows the minds and hearts of humans from the beginning of their existence they take joy in other people's deaths. They like to see other people suffer. They like to see people in agony, especially people that are out there doing good—they always want to stop them. Apostle John said that people like darkness more than light because their work is evil.

During those days, in Roman and Greek arenas, people would be shouting and cheering as gladiators fought and killed one another, or as animals, such as lions, tore humans apart. People were right there on the day of crucifixion. They watched Christ on the Cross.

And they scornfully said, "He saved others," they said, "but he can't save himself! He's the king of Israel! Let him come down now from the Cross, and we will believe in him." Matt 27:42.

They were mocking the Creator of the universe as he was nailed to the Cross. It continues even today in some countries where the persecution of Christians is their main goal.

It also continues in our society today on television and in some movies, where they encourage and promote violence, where people plan to kill and torture each other, and they show destruction and all forms of immorality that cause emotional and mental violence in the human heart, and sometimes even death.

## The Cross and the Crucifixion

> *"Our Lord Jesus Christ died on the Cross to bring forth love and compassion."*

Our Lord Jesus Christ died on the Cross to bring forth love and compassion. He wants us to know that sin's impact on human life brings all other evil into our world, from one society to another society, from one culture to another.

When one country plans to wipe out another country off of the face of the earth, many people stand there, listening to that statement, very happy and rejoicing.

It is the responsibility of believers to teach and guide their children, grandchildren, relatives, and families against all influences of evil and violence. The paradise that our Lord mentioned on the Cross means heaven. Jesus teaches us that, after death, the saved believers go straight to heaven.

# 2

# The Foreknowledge of God

God, in His omniscience, knows what the future holds for both individuals and for nations. God knows and sees everything in advance, and His will is carried out in accordance with His plans and purposes. In the Old Testament and in the New Testament, God's foreknowledge never changes.

> "*God's will is carried out in accordance with His plans and purposes.*"

The foreknowledge of God is related to or connected to election and predestination. God is the one and only Creator, and He is the sole ruler of the universe. God is the all-knowing Creator. God knows everything. He knew about you and me before we entered our mother's wombs, and before we arrived here on earth.

## The Cross and the Crucifixion

The psalmist says: "You have searched me, LORD, and you know me. You know when I sit and when I rise; you perceive my thoughts from afar. You discern my going out and my lying down; you are familiar with all my ways. Before a word is on my tongue you, LORD, know it completely." Psalm 139:1-4.

This psalm explains all of the attributes of God, especially His omnipresence and His omniscience, which are God's supernatural way of caring for His children. God, the Creator of heaven and earth who created us, knows us more than we know ourselves.

God is always present. God has never been far away from His people, especially from those who are calling unto Him, day and night.

> *"Almighty God knows our inward, innermost thoughts, motives, fears, and all our hearts' desires."*

God's mercy is always upon us in any circumstances upon individuals, upon nations, and upon the entire world. He knows our inward, innermost thoughts, motives, fears, and all our hearts' desires. God knows all our outward behaviors and our actions.

He knows everything about us—what we do from the minute we wake up in the morning until the end of the day. God, in His mercy, encircles us with His infinite care, favor, and love.

We, as children of God, cannot go anywhere beyond His reach. He guides and leads us with His mighty strength. He always makes sure that He brings what He has started in our lives to completion, with His love and power.

> *"Everyone in this universe has a purpose and an assignment related to what they need to do for the welfare of the people in the world."*

God is creatively and actively involved with every individual and with the universe. Everyone in this universe has a purpose and an assignment related to what they need to do for the welfare of the people in the world. Every individual is here to do good and live good lives with themselves and with others.

The psalmist stated that God ordained the time of our lives. This means that God knows when we will come back to Him—down to the very minute. "The time of God" refers back to God's plan for individuals on earth, and for all people in the world.

God does not want anyone to perish. This means that He does not want anyone leave this earth without knowing or worshipping Him.

He wants us to repent our sins and turn back to Him. God is a merciful and mighty God. He does not treat us according to our iniquities. We must know that

## The Cross and the Crucifixion

Jesus Christ is the only way to heaven. He is the way, the truth, and the life. We are comforted through the power of the indwelling of the Holy Spirit, knowing that God constantly knows our needs, whether medical or financial.

> *"God knows all of our troubles and sufferings, and He has already planned the way of escape for us through forgiveness, salvation, and sanctification."*

God knows all of our troubles and sufferings, and He has already planned the way of escape for us through forgiveness, salvation, and sanctification. His thought is unfathomable, immeasurable, and unspeakable.

The Bible says: "However, as it is written: 'What no eye has seen, what no ear has heard, and what no human mind has conceived"—the things God has prepared for those who love him." 1 Cor 2:9.

We must meditate on God's love for us, so that we can abide in Him more and more. The psalmist meditated on God's great love for him throughout his life. He loves the Lord greatly and remembers how close God has been to him.

Christians need to always meditate on God's love, mercy, protection, and provisions for us. We have seen the Lord's mercy salvation, love, goodness, truth, and grace.

We should greatly appreciate God's presence and stay away from earthly things that can contaminate us. Believers must pray at all times in order to do what is acceptable in His sight. We must pray that God will wash us clean from any unrighteousness at all times throughout our lives.

It is very important to know the power of the Cross. It is impossible to overlook the fact that the Cross is at the center of the New Testament's theology of salvation and that it is also the starting point of Christian theology.

The Cross of Christ shows us and leads us to the full knowledge by which we may finally and fully understand and appreciate the work of Christ on our behalf.

> "*Christians need to always meditate on God's love, mercy, protection, and provisions for us.*"

The gospel of Mark indicated that it is at the Cross that Jesus Christ was recognized as God's divinely appointed Savior of the world. "Just as the Son of Man did not come to be served, but to serve, and to give his life as a ransom for many." Matt 20:28.

"And when the centurion, who stood there in front of Jesus, saw how he died, he said, "Surely this man was the Son of God!" Mark 15:39.

## The Cross and the Crucifixion

"Ransom means a price paid to obtain the freedom of others or the price paid to heal the sick in hospitals –but, instead, this is sin—sickness.

Our Lord gave us the parable of the man who fell among the thieves: "In reply Jesus said: 'A man was going down from Jerusalem to Jericho, when he was attacked by robbers. They stripped him of his clothes, beat him and went away, leaving him half dead.'" Luke 10:30.

In Jesus' redemptive work, He paid the price to release individuals and all people of the universe from the dominion of sin, with his death.

Christ releases us from sin's condemnation: "Therefore, there is now no condemnation for those who are in Christ Jesus." Rom 8:1. The death of Christ carried a broader and deeper significance in the lives of believers.

> "Without the Cross, we would have to die for our sins. Christ's Cross is the visible attribute of the work of God the Father in Christ Jesus."

The Cross is a symbol of God's actions in Christ, a motivator, on the Cross, where our salvation was completed. Without the Cross, we would have to die for our sins. Christ's Cross is the visible attribute of the work of God the Father in Christ Jesus.

## The Cross and the Crucifixion

The Cross of Christ is where we see God's reconciliation of the world with Himself: "God was reconciling the world to himself in Christ, not counting people's sins against them. And he has committed to us the message of reconciliation." 2 Cor 5:19.

Christ's Cross is the power of God. Apostle Paul stated, "For the message of the Cross is foolishness to those who are perishing, but to us who are being saved it is the power of God." 1 Cor 1:18.

Paul said that the message of the Cross involved wisdom and truth, and that it showed that God actively came to the earth to save and redeem us from the power of sin and death, which is foolishness to some people.

> *"Thanks be to God the Father that His foolishness, weakness, and long-suffering in Christ's crucifixion provided salvation for the problem of sin."*

The supposed wisdom of the world has excluded God from everything. It praises human self-righteousness and humanity above all and it refuses to acknowledge God—this is pure foolishness. All believers must emphasize the word of God and the revelation of the Cross. The gospel message of the Cross has never been recognized by science, philosophy, or any other human wisdom.

The message of the crucifixion and resurrection of Christ, in the world's view, is foolishness. Thanks be

## The Cross and the Crucifixion

to God the Father that His foolishness, weakness, and longsuffering in Christ's crucifixion provided salvation for the problem of sin, which has baffled the people of the world throughout human history. God's power, standards, plans, and values are different from those of the people of the world.

The power and wisdom of God through Christ and the power of the Cross through the Holy Spirit produce spirited growth in humanity, changing and canceling the things of the world of present or new ages.

Through Jesus Christ's crucifixion and resurrection, God continues to nullify the honored things of this present age. One day, when Christ returns, He will bring all worldly systems to an end.

*"It is through Christ, in Christ, and with Christ Jesus, that the entire body of Christ receives wisdom from God."*

It is through Christ, in Christ, and with Christ Jesus, that the entire body of Christ receives wisdom from God. Through Christ, we experience righteousness, sanctification, and redemption.

As long as we abide and trust in Jesus Christ, He is the source of all blessings. He is the channel of all blessings. He is the fountain of all blessings. We must remain in Him.

Believers must focus on the truth of the Gospel, which is redemption through Jesus Christ, based on the power of the Holy Spirit. The connection of the Cross with God's wisdom and power is very amazing.

Most significant, is the connection of Christ's Cross itself, "We preach Christ crucified: a stumbling block to Jews and foolishness to Gentiles, but to those whom God has called, both Jews and Greeks, Christ the power of God and the wisdom of God." 1 Cor 1:23-24.

> *"Christ humbles Himself by making Himself a servant to the sick and to the poor. He is always ready to fulfill their requests and He goes through different pains to serve them."*

Christ humbles Himself by making Himself a servant to the sick and to the poor. He is always ready to fulfill their requests and He goes through different pains to serve them. There has never been an example of usefulness and beneficence like in the death of Christ.

He lived as a servant and went about doing good, but he died on the Cross as a sacrifice. In doing so, He did the greatest good of all. He came to the world with a purpose, which was to give His life as a ransom for many. This is a good reason why we should not strive for any earthly positions, because Christ is our banner.

## The Cross and the Crucifixion

We should study to do good for Christ, who is all-sufficient. The people of Jesus' days did not understand how Christ's death, which was a sign of weakness and failure, could ever solve their problems.

The structure of this sentence equates Christ's crucifixion: Christ is the power and wisdom of God. Therefore, the Cross is seen as a defining revelation of who Christ is—the coming Messiah who is the wisdom and power of God, mentioned in the Old Testament.

> *"The Cross is seen as God's deliberate choice and plan. God did not just allow it. It was not by accident."*

The Cross is seen as God's deliberate choice and plan. God did not just allow it. It was not by accident. Rather, God chose the weak and foolish things of this earth and deliberately used them to confound the wise and to shame the strong. God's character is demonstrated through the Cross to show God's love for the despised things of the world.

The Cross is a symbol of shame in the Old Testament: "You must not leave the body hanging on the pole overnight. Be sure to bury it that same day, because anyone who is hung on a pole is under God's curse. You must not desecrate the land the LORD your God is giving you as an inheritance." Deut 21:23.

Also, "Christ redeemed us from the curse of the law by becoming a curse for us, for it is written: 'Cursed is everyone who is hung on a pole.' He redeemed us in order that the blessing given to Abraham might come to the Gentiles through Christ Jesus, so that by faith we might receive the promise of the Spirit." Gal 3:13-14.

> *"We Christians were able to receive the promise of the power of the Holy Spirit, through faith in his life and through the power of the Spirit."*

We Christians, all believers, were redeemed from the curse of sin and the law. We have received the blessings of Abraham through the finished redemptive work of Jesus Christ.

As a result, we were able to receive the promise of the power of the Holy Spirit, through faith in his life and through the power of the Spirit.

The Cross is the tool for the redemption of human kind. This fact is essential and final to any theology of the Cross. Nevertheless, the imagery used to discuss the Cross has been highly disputed.

The Cross is displayed as a sacrifice of atonement in: "All are justified freely by his grace through the redemption that came by Christ Jesus" Rom 3:24.

The sacrifice and death of animals in the Old Testament are two major connections to this metaphor of the Cross. The first is the wrath of God and the second is salvation through the redemptive sacrifice of Christ.

The "wrath of God" means that God's spirit grieved because of the continuous increase of evil in the world. Men and women are kept from their rightful place as God's highest and most prized possessions.

> *"Those who have faith in Christ must live their lives in intimate relationships with the Lord, both in His death and in His resurrection."*

The Cross of Christ paid the penalty for the sins of humanity and, therefore, it serves to free humans from sin and death and allows them to live and worship God. The Cross of Christ speaks to the nature of Christian life:

"I have been crucified with Christ and I no longer live, but Christ lives in me. The life I now live in the body, I live by faith in the Son of God, who loved me and gave himself for me." Gal 2:20.

Paul's relationship with Christ consisted of his profound personal attachment and reliance upon the Lord.

This is the case with all believers today. Those who have faith in Christ must live their lives in intimate relationships with the Lord, both in His death and in His resurrection. All believers have been crucified with Christ on the Cross.

Believers have become dead to the law as a means of salvation and live through Christ for God. Because of salvation in Christ, sin and temptation no longer has control over them. They now live with Christ and in His resurrection. Christ and his strength live within believers. Christ has become the source of all life and the center of all our thoughts, words, and deeds.

> *"Living by faith can be seen in all believers living in the Spirit."*

It is through the Holy Spirit that Christ's risen life continually communicates with us. Believers sharing in Christ's death and resurrection are appropriated through faith. We confidently believe in Christ's love and devotion, and we are loyal to the Son of God, who loved us and gave Himself for us. Living by faith can be seen in all believers living in the Spirit.

The Cross is as central to living a Christian life as it is to entering into life itself: "May I never boast except in the Cross of our Lord Jesus Christ, through which the world has been crucified to me, and I to the world." Gal 6:14.

The Cross of Christ, representing the horrible death that the Savior suffered for mankind's eternal salvation, is now the barrier by which the world is separated from believers and believers from the world. There will be no sharing in the salvation and glory of

## The Cross and the Crucifixion

Christ's Cross for believers who have not turned around completely from all earthly pleasures and things that contaminate them and draw their hearts away from Christ.

Through the power of the Cross, Christ became sin for us. He took the blame and burned in the wrath for us. We stand forgiven at the Cross of the Son of God who was slain for us. The Cross divided the world into two. A believer in Jesus needs the message of the Cross daily. Old Testament sacrifices pointed to Jesus' work of redemption on the Cross.

John the Baptist said to Jesus: "Look, the Lamb of God, who takes away the sin of the world!" John 1:29. Jesus said "It is finished." He completed the work that the Father assigned to Him.

> *"God willingly offered His Son to suffer and die to provide forgiveness and justification for us."*

Jesus suffered and died to take away the wrath of God. God is a God of wrath and love. God demanded that His one and only begotten Son suffer and die for you and me. God willingly offered His Son to suffer and die to provide forgiveness and justification for us: "Since we have now been justified by his blood, how much more shall we be saved from God's wrath through him!" Rom 5:9.

The power of the Cross is the Gospel that saves and transforms. God saves us from the consequences of sin and prevents further expressions of sin from coming to life within us. The Cross of Christ is a tool for reconciliation. The Cross of Jesus Christ helps sinners to repent.

It is a source of power that canceled sins completely, has the power to dethrone sin from the heart, and helps them to live a new and holy life. His suffering on the Cross removed the guilt of sin from the lives of God's children.

> *"The power of the Cross is so great that it sets sinners free from the power of sin."*

The children of God are washed by the blood of the Lamb. The power of the Cross is so great that it sets sinners free from the power of sin: "For I am not ashamed of the gospel, because it is the power of God that brings salvation to everyone who believes: first to the Jew, then to the Gentile." Rom 1:16.

As we are free from sin and alive in righteousness: "In the same way, count yourselves dead to sin but alive to God in Christ Jesus." Rom 6:11.

As we are still in the flesh, sin still wages war against us by tempting us and enticing us with some of the things of the world. But because of the power of the Cross of Jesus Christ, sin cannot and will not have dominion over us.

## The Cross and the Crucifixion

Because there is power in the Cross of Jesus, there is power in the blood of Jesus power for life and for being holy, because He said, "Be Holy because I am Holy." 1 Peter 1:16. The power of the Cross is the only real power that helps people deliver sinners from their sins and deliver their souls from sin and death.

*"The power of the Cross is a liberating power from the bondage and enslavement of sin."*

The power of the Cross brings about repentance from evil, hate, jealousy, immoral life styles, lust, and all the things of the world that contaminate the spirit, the soul, and the body of the human race. The power of the Cross is a liberating power from the bondage and enslavement of sin.

The power of the Cross of Christ frees sinners, the lost, and all of the children of God from sin and sinful natures so that they may live lives that are pleasing to God.

Jesus Christ went to the Cross with the mighty power of love to release us from the power of sin and death. In the Old Testament, God delivered the children of Israel from slavery in Egypt, with a powerful hand. In the same way, Jesus Christ delivered the people of the entire world from their sin, the sin that had enslaved and tormented them for years.

## The Cross and the Crucifixion

Therefore, with His mighty arms stretched, God the Father, through Jesus Christ, His only begotten Son, delivered the Jews and Gentiles from the curse of the sin of Adam and Eve. Christ does not want anyone to perish. He wants everyone to gain knowledge of repentance and to pray for forgiveness, which comes from Him.

Therefore, the Cross was a complete sacrifice for our sins. The Cross of Christ redeemed each and every living soul on earth. "For you granted him authority over all people that he might give eternal life to all those you have given him . . . While I was with them, I protected them and kept them safe by that name you gave me. None has been lost except the one doomed to destruction so that Scripture would be fulfilled." John 17:2, 12.

> *"Jesus was there for us in our place. God the Father placed all our sins, penalties, and punishment on His Son Jesus on the Cross."*

The sins of all humanity were nailed on Jesus Christ on the Cross. He was there for us in our place. God the Father placed all our sins, penalties, and punishment on His Son Jesus on the Cross.

The angel Gabriel stated that Jesus would deliver His people from their sins: "She will give birth to a son, and you are to give him the name Jesus, because he will save his people from their sins." Matt 1:21. Joseph had a dream and the angel of the Lord spoke to him concerning his betrothal to his wife Mary.

*"Through the power of the Cross, the Holy Spirit produces the fruit of faith in the hearts of people so that they can believe in Jesus."*

Through the power of the Cross, the Holy Spirit produces the fruit of faith in the hearts of people so that they can believe in Jesus. The blood of Jesus Christ cleanses and purges away all unrighteousness.

The Cross of Christ is so powerful that it delivers sinners from fear, violence, jealousy, evil thoughts, and from all kinds of immoral lifestyles that destroy the people and children of God.

On the Cross, God the Son showed us, through His mercy and grace, that our sins had been washed clean on the Cross. The Cross of Christ's power delivered us from the power of sin, death, and the grave.

We forever belong to Jesus. Sin has no dominion over us. Death has been swallowed up in the victory. The Cross of Christ renews our will to be the same as God's will for our lives.

We will hate all worldly things that are sinful and we will love godly things that are holy, through the power of the indwelling of the Holy Spirit. The Holy Spirit that the Father sent, which dwells in our hearts, produces and works through us to free us from the dominion of sin. The Cross brought us out of the slavery of sin and set us free so that we may serve the Lord with singleness of heart.

# 3

# The First Adam and the Second Adam

We have to also connect and contrast the first Adam who committed sin in the Garden of Eden and whose sin affected the entire human race. Our Lord and Savior Jesus were in the Garden of Gethsemane to change the curse of the sin of Adam.

> "*Christ paid it all. We owe it all to Him. He washed away our sins with His precious blood on the Cross. Sin's wages have been paid in full.*"

The second Adam, a Spirit-being, was ready to sacrifice Himself for the sins of all humanity. He sacrificed himself forever for our sins. Christ paid it all. We owe it all to Him. He washed away our sins with His precious blood on the Cross. Sin's wages have been paid in full.

His Father will never forsake Him anymore. There is nothing more to be done or required for sinners' salvation on the Cross: "But when this priest had offered for all time one sacrifice for sins, he sat down at the right hand of God." Heb 10:12.

> *"The gift of grace is free and by His stripes we are healed. The Cross is God's purpose."*

Christ offered one sacrifice for all sins forever. He sat down at the right hand of God the Father, pleading our cases and praying for us. There is nothing we can do. The gift of grace is free and by His stripes we are healed. The Cross is God's purpose.

He announced it to the prophet Isaiah many years before its fulfillment: "We all, like sheep, have gone astray, each of us has turned to our own way; and the LORD has laid on him the iniquity of us all." Isa 53:6.

God the Father offered His justice against sin and His mercy and grace to sinners. The Cross is the sign of salvation for all people in the world. God fulfills what He said when Adam and Eve fell into sin in the Garden of Eden, "And I will put enmity between you and the woman, and between your offspring and hers; he will crush your head, and you will strike his heel." Gen 3:15.

Jesus' death and resurrection made many people in the world, who were spiritually dead, alive in Him.

He called them to worship God and will continue to revive dead souls and make them alive in Him. Christ is the God of all living souls on earth. God's purpose was achieved just as he had planned it.

Moreover, God's love was manifested in the hearts of people in the world. Satan's power over the people of the world was destroyed and will be destroyed completely when Christ returns. Sin's power of condemnation has been done away with completely in the lives of those who believe in Christ and his resurrection. Believers were able to receive their inheritance as the adopted children of God through Jesus Christ our Savior.

> *"The Cross is where God the Father did all the work of reconciliation and redemption."*

Christ carried our past, present, and future sins on the Cross. On the Cross, the ministry of reconciliation was reached. Christ reconciled us with God, through His atoning sacrifice. The Cross is where God the Father did all the work of reconciliation and redemption.

We are justified by His grace through the redemption of our Lord Jesus Christ, whom God the Father sent as propitiation for our sin, by having faith in His Son. There are many ways available for believers through the power of the blood of Christ our Lord.

Reconciliation is, naturally, the first blessing and is among the things that sinners must do—those who willingly desire a share in the work of redemption through or by participating in other blessings of redemption.

> *Believers who have already received the blessing of reconciliation should obtain a deeper reconciliation and a more spiritual concept of blessedness.*

Believers who have already received the blessing of reconciliation should obtain a deeper reconciliation and a more spiritual concept of blessedness. The power of reconciliation is rooted in redemption. A fuller knowledge of reconciliation is a means by which to receive the power of the blood of Christ.

# 4

## "Father, Forgive Them; for They Do Not Know What They Are Doing."
### Luke 23:34

Jesus' forgiveness was not only for the Romans and people of His day. Jesus' forgiveness spread to all of the people of the earth. His forgiveness continues to reach undeserving sinners today. God's forgiveness through Jesus Christ, His Son, comes to those who don't know what they are doing, even today.

In the Old Testament, God extended His forgiveness to individual men and women, and to an entire nation. For example, God forgave the nation of Israel and restored them back to their land. Divine forgiveness is when God restores a sinner back to his or her relationship with Him. The removal of guilt is very important, therefore, to forgive the offense against God's holiness.

> *"There is no greater gift than the divine gift of grace. Nothing can be offered to humanity that is greater than the gift of grace to know that your sins are forever forgiven."*

Christ grants us the remission of sins. The risen and exalted Lord forgives us all our sins. There is no greater gift than the divine gift of grace. Nothing can be offered to humanity that is greater than the gift of grace to know that your sins are forever forgiven.

Thus, we are at peace with ourselves and with God the Father, and we are focused on the good news of the Gospel. The most important aspect is that there must be repentance of sin. Without such a change of mind regarding our sins and our relationship to be able to stand before our maker, God, the ruler of human souls, there will be no salvation.

The key tools are to repent, to ask for forgiveness of your sins, and to receive the gift of grace to salvation. Through repentance and faith, the way to salvation is open because, by faith, the hearts of all who believe in Christ are cleansed by this blood of the Lamb and by the Holy Spirit who sanctified the believer.

## The Cross and the Crucifixion

Our Lord Jesus was going through agony with the crown of thorns on His head and his body was bruised with strips of beating, but He pleaded with the Father to forgive us because we didn't know what we were doing. In the sorrowful agony of death, our Lord suffered unimaginable pain on His body and on His head, but He still showed us mercy.

> *"God, in His mercy and love, personally experienced the pain of the sacrificial Lamb that satisfied His divine justice, in order to forgive us our sins and to open the gates of heaven for eternal life."*

God, in His mercy and love, personally experienced the pain of the sacrificial Lamb that satisfied His divine justice, in order to forgive us our sins and to open the gates of heaven for eternal life.

Our Lord suffered humiliation from the people who were mocking Him when He was on the Cross. When the solder pierced His side, blood and water flowed, symbolizing His mercy and grace.

During His dedication in the Temple when He was born, prophet Simeon gave a revelation of Christ suffering, which Mary kept in her heart and pondered on it from time to time: "Then Simeon blessed them and said to Mary, his mother: 'This child is destined to cause the falling and rising of many in Israel, and to be a sign that will be spoken against, so that the thoughts of many hearts will be revealed. And a sword will pierce your own soul too.'" Luke 2:34-35.

Christ died on the Cross for us. We are cleansed from all wickedness, from every last sin. We are one with the Father, the Son, and the Holy Spirit, as His children. We are free to boldly and confidently approach the throne of grace with any of our problems, troubles, or needs.

The forgiveness of God through Jesus Christ is not only for people who do not know what they are doing. God's forgiveness of sin also applies to those who knowingly do what is wrong to others and to those who intentionally hurt their fellow citizens.

God, through Jesus Christ, washed away our past, present, and future sins with the redemptive work of Jesus Christ on the Cross.

> *"It is not by our works or by the money we give to the church or to the needy, but by His grace that He saved us."*

It is not by our works or by the money we give to the church or to the needy, but by His grace that He saved us. By His stripes, we are healed. He laid down His life so that He could give us His life in return. Jesus has completed the work of redemption. He has redeemed us from sin and death.

## The Cross and the Crucifixion

Our Lord suffered and took the sins of Israel, as well as the sins of the whole world, unto himself. The physical death of Jesus Christ on the Cross is the central theme from which all true Christianity is based. Without the physical death on the Cross, there would be no Christianity and there would be no salvation.

We would have died because of our sins. There would have been no heaven for anyone to go to or enter. Our Lord came to this earth specifically to save sinners through His suffering.

> *"The message of Jesus Christ, His redeeming love, death, and resurrection serve as the foundational truth of all Christians."*

The message of Jesus Christ, His redeeming love, death, and resurrection serve as the foundational truth of all Christians. For example, look at our salvation and the gift and power of the Holy Spirit in our lives.

Whenever the power of humanity is revealed and accomplished, believers must rise to the understanding of God the Father's infinite love that goes straight to believers' souls. Jesus is the God of love, grace, and compassion. Our Lord's suffering reveals Christ's hidden disposition either towards good or evil.

The forgiveness of sins is offered to those who believe in His death and His atoning sacrifice. Death came through Adam and life came through Christ: "For if by one man's offence death reigned by one; much more they which receive abundance of grace and of the gift of righteousness shall reign in life by one Jesus Christ.

> "*The forgiveness of sins is offered to those who believe in His death and His atoning sacrifice.*"

"For if, by the trespass of the one man, death reigned through that one man, how much more will those who receive God's abundant provision of grace and of the gift of righteousness reign in life through the one man, Jesus Christ!

Consequently, just as one trespass resulted in condemnation for all people, so also one righteous act resulted in justification and life for all people." Rom 5:17-18.

# 5

# "Jesus Answered Him, 'Truly I Tell You, Today You Will Be with Me in Paradise.'"
### Luke 23:43

The thief on Christ's side said, "Remember me when you come to your Kingdom." Jesus' reply gives us assurance that it is never too late to repent and pray for forgiveness, up to the very last minute of our life on earth.

> *"Jesus has been saying to all people on earth, from that moment on the Cross, that it is never too late to ask for forgiveness of sin from our sin-bearer, Jesus Christ."*

Jesus has been saying to all people on earth, from that moment on the Cross, that it is never too late to ask for forgiveness of sin from our sin-bearer, Jesus

Christ. The words Jesus spoke in Luke. 23:43 were words of comfort to the thief on his right side. We have to see the Garden of Eden as the first paradise. "Now the LORD God had planted a garden in the east, in Eden; and there he put the man he had formed." Gen 2:8.

We must also see: "And I know that this man—whether in the body or apart from the body I do not know, but God knows—was caught up to paradise and heard inexpressible things, things that no one is permitted to tell." 2 Cor 12:3-4.

> *"Our Lord assured the thief a life in Him, that he was going to a place of blessings, better than what he was missing on earth."*

Our Lord assured the thief a life in Him, that he was going to a place of blessings, better than what he was missing on earth. He assured him that, compared to his present life on earth, he would be happier after his death and that his soul would be separated from his body, though his body was on the Cross.

Even today, the soul of a righteous person will be made very happy after death. He will be with Jesus forever. We also must put ourselves in a position where the Lord will be able to remember us and bless us.

Then, Jesus will not only remember, but He will also bless us with His gift of grace, abundant grace to those who believe in Him. He saved the thief when we thought that all the power of the Savior had left Him. Jesus Christ's power was known to the soldiers when darkness filled the earth.

It came before the dark overshadowing of the land. It came before the great earthquake that shook violently, and some of the graves opened and saints walked out of the graves and visited their relatives in Jerusalem.

> *"Jesus has the power to save sinners and wash them clean with His blood because that is the reason why He came to the world."*

Jesus was on the Cross exercising His infinite power over all of His created beings: "Therefore he is able to save completely those who come to God through him, because he always lives to intercede for them." Heb 7:25.

Jesus has the power to save sinners and wash them clean with His blood because that is the reason why He came to the world. Jesus' power is immeasurable and incomparable: "In him we have redemption through his blood, the forgiveness of sins, in accordance with the riches of God's grace." Eph 1:7.

Jesus continued to stay on the Cross in order to redeem the soul of the thief. Christ was on the Cross for the thief, for you, and for me until He gave up the

## The Cross and the Crucifixion

ghost. We must come to the Lord in order to live a life that will bring glory to His Holy name and with strong faith that we will be with Him in heaven.

> *"Believers see Christ and the Cross clearly as the only way to salvation, forgiveness of sins, resurrection of the body, and life everlasting."*

Believers see Christ and the Cross clearly as the only way to salvation, forgiveness of sins, resurrection of the body, and life everlasting.

When Christ prayed for forgiveness on the Cross to show that the Father heard Him and answered that prayer, His prayer for the thief was answered. The thief who never knew Him cried out to Him, that He should remember him.

Words of love and mercy came out of the mouth of Christ and He said, "Jesus answered him, 'Truly I tell you, today you will be with me in paradise.'" Luke 23:43.

Jesus, from the Cross, proclaimed the word of the Gospel of God to the sinner. He forgave a murderer who was crucified on the Cross with Him. Christ was in the middle of the two malefactors who were crucified with Him. This is the fulfillment of prophet Isaiah both thieves were murderers.

Jesus Christ went to the Cross to take away the wrath of God from all those who God the Father has given to Him. The God's grace given to the thief had led him to repent and confess to the Lord, "We are punished justly, for we are getting what our deeds deserve. But this man has done nothing wrong." Luke 23:41.

God's grace in him made him speak boldly about his sin, and to cry out to Jesus to remember him in His kingdom. Jesus Christ had mercy upon him and brought him to repentance so that by faith he could receive eternal life. It was the Cross of Christ that God used to open the thief's heart to salvation and repentance.

> *"The power of the Cross and with Jesus hanging on it and the power of God the Father Almighty planned the work of redemption unto salvation."*

The power of the Cross and with Jesus hanging on it and the power of God the Father Almighty planned the work of redemption unto salvation.

# 6

# "Woman, Here Is Your Son ... Here Is Your Mother."
### John 19:26-27

These words came from Jesus on the Cross where He was hanging during His final hours on earth, "When Jesus saw his mother there, and the disciple whom he loved standing nearby, he said to her, 'Woman, here is your son,' and to the disciple, 'Here is your mother.' From that time on, this disciple took her into his home." John 19:26-27.

Mary and the other women were standing by the Cross, full of sorrow, with the disciples that Jesus loved. Christ meant that His mother should be part of John's family that John should be part of Mary's family, and they should become the first body of Christ or family of God.

He meant a spiritual connection—this was revealed by Jesus on the Cross. Therefore, even today, all believers are one in the Lord. We share the same Spirit, the Spirit of Christ. At the same time, Jesus separated Himself from the earthly part of Him, which tied Him and His mother together. It dissolved in that moment on the Cross because Christ was ready to put on His divine attribute. Mary, the mother of God, was the last aspect of His humanity.

Christ knew that His human status as Son would soon come to an end. The Cross, through the power of the Holy Spirit, took off the body of flesh of Jesus and separated Him from His mother. This brought Mary to the realization of Simeon's prophecy that said: "And a sword will pierce your own soul too." Luke 2:35.

> "*Standing and gazing at the Cross, believers must be reassured that God the Father, through Jesus Christ, His Son, in the power of the Holy Spirit, loves humanity.*"

Jesus was concerned about His mother, even though He was in agony to the point of death. He made caring provisions for His mother, and gave responsibility of His mother to His beloved disciple, to help Him to take care of His mother.

Standing and gazing at the Cross, believers must be reassured that God the Father, through Jesus Christ, His Son, in the power of the Holy Spirit, loves humanity. Christ loves His people for whom He suffered to save.

This shows us that we must try our best to provide for our parents, making provisions in case anything should happen to us, so that our mothers will have something to live on and someone to care for them. Jesus loved His mother and He loved her to the end.

> *"Believers should meditate on this love of Christ towards His mother at the end and do the same for our loved ones."*

Believers should meditate on this love of Christ towards His mother at the end and do the same for our loved ones. Christ suffered for our sins in order to redeem us from our sins. Believers should be grateful for the love of Christ that brings salvation to the world. Christ showed His love for people and His mother to the end.

During His agony on the Cross while He was dying, Jesus Christ showed that He was concerned about the welfare of His mother. He appointed the disciple whom He loved to take care of His mother to assist her and the entire family.

As believers of Christ, we have to imitate Christ, help the needy among us, care for our family and friends, and take responsibility for our elderly, senior citizens until the last hour of their lives. What we must learn here, in Jesus' statement to His mother, is the emphasis on taking responsibility for our dependent parents.

> *"If any earthly troubles take us away from our responsibility of caring for our parents, we must delegate the responsibility to someone else on our behalf."*

If any earthly troubles take us away from our responsibility of caring for our parents, we must delegate the responsibility to someone else on our behalf who can take care of our senior citizens and elderly parents.

Mary, His mother, John's mother, Mary Magdalene, Joanna, Mary the mother of James, and Mary the wife of Cleophas who was Jesus' earthly Father's brother were at the Cross, along with other women who were with them. The Bible says, "Near the Cross of Jesus stood his mother." John 19:25.

His mother was at the foot of the Cross with eyes full of love, remembering what Simeon the prophet had told her during His dedication in the temple. With these words in her remembrance, Mary offered prayer and praises to God, with all her heart.

At that time on the Cross, Christ had already separated Himself, from Mary and all earthly things. He had to break the mother-son relationship because He was on the Cross for the sins of the whole world.

Just as He left His glory in heaven and became human, leaving His Father's glory as God the Son in heaven, the same Christ called His mother "woman" because He was taking on the sin of the whole world and would soon go back to heaven in His glory.

Mary was a born-again Christian, just like any of us today. We are all sinners saved by the grace of God through Jesus Christ, our Lord. Mary went through the Cross, through the blood of Jesus, for her salvation. Christ called Mary "woman" because He was Mary's Savior, just as He is our Savior today.

> *"Jesus Christ is our predestination, justification, reconciliation, and propitiation for our sins and for the sins of all humanity."*

Jesus Christ is our predestination, justification, reconciliation, and propitiation for our sins and for the sins of all humanity. Jesus Christ died and arose for the sins of you and me, as well as for the sins of Mary, His earthly mother. Jesus loved His mother, as He loved everyone on this earth, and, at that moment, He assigned the responsibility of caring for His mother to John. He wanted John to see that Mary's life would continue after His ascension to heaven.

> "Believers are also substitutes for Christ in the world. We must do all that is necessary to reach sinners and the lost."

Jesus Christ took all of humanity's sins upon Him on the Cross. He is our substitute. He took our place. Christ is the Redeemer King. Believers are also substitutes for Christ in the world. We must do all that is necessary to reach sinners and the lost, going to the ends of the earth because this is what Christ would do if He were in the world today. Christ gave us His Spirit. His hands are our hands, His feet are our feet, and his eyes are our eyes. We must lead the hardest sinners unto Him.

# 7

# "Eloi, Eloi, Lema Sabachthani? My God, My God, Why Have You Forsaken Me?"
### Mark 15:34

Christ struggled mightily with Satan, sin, and death on the Cross all three of these are curses of God and His body was tormented hanging on the Cross. He cried with a loud voice up to the point that the veil of the Temple was rent into two.

God sent His only Son to sacrifice Himself for our sins. Indirectly, He sent Himself as a human with divine nature, as divine nature living in a human body. Christ had His Father's divine nature, which was how He was able to be perfect in order to be our final sacrifice.

The words in this verse also mean that Jesus Christ was the Lamb of God who took away the sins of the whole world. He gave His life as a ransom for many. As He said, He finished the work that the Father gave Him to do.

The judgment of God came upon the earth and the temple curtain was turned upside down. Christ said, "My God, my God, why have you forsaken me?" At that time, Jesus Christ took the human side of us. The Father laid all of our sins on Him and turned His back on His Son in order for Him to carry our sins.

> "*Christ carried all our guilt upon Him. He was made accountable for the sins of all people. He bore the sins of all people on the Cross.*"

"Eloi" signifies strength, the name of the Almighty God. Christ called out the name of God because He was in a sinner's position at that time. Christ did not say, "my Father," because, at that time, Christ took our position.

This expression denotes the intense suffering that Christ was going through at that particular hour on the Cross the great bodily suffering on the Cross where the Son of God was crucified for the sins of the whole world.

## The Cross and the Crucifixion

Christ carried all our guilt upon Him. He was made accountable for the sins of all people. He bore the sins of all people on the Cross. He fulfilled the mission that He came to earth to do, and the Father approved of it. God hates sin and the sight of sin.

> *"Christ fulfilled the mission that He came to earth to do, and the Father approved of it. God hates sin and the sight of sin."*

God sent Adam and Eve out of the Garden of Eden because of their sin: "So the LORD God banished him from the Garden of Eden to work the ground from which he had been taken." Gen 3:23.

God also dealt with the wickedness of people in the world during Noah's time, when the evil of humans on earth was so great. He judged them with flood waters, "But Noah found favor in the eyes of the LORD." Gen 6:8.

God continues to judge the wickedness of people with so many adversities even today. God is the God of love but He does not allow injustice or wickedness in the lives of His people. Suffering and death formed a part of the Messiah from the beginning. They are part of His divine nature. He knew the price He had to pay in order to redeem us from our sin.

Christ cried aloud "My God, my God." This was the human side of Him acknowledging and confirming what He had done for us on the Cross, which was the sacrifice of Himself. In the garden of Gethsemane, Jesus willingly put His mind in a state of separation from God and saw himself in this illusion as powerless.

Jesus demonstrated the truth of the power of His oneness and our oneness with God. He demonstrated what the separation looks like for us, as well as its disempowering effects. Through our oneness with the divine Spirit, the truth of who we really are will be resurrected.

> *"We must be like Christ. Christ gave up His spirit for you and me. Christ sacrificed His life as the Passover Lamb for us."*

The ongoing application of the Cross in our lives has to do with the application of the Cross in our lives. It has to do with embracing the exchange that God has for us in terms of nature. We must be like Christ. Christ gave up His spirit for you and me. Christ sacrificed His life as the Passover Lamb for us.

# 8

# "I Am Thirsty."
## John 19:28

Christ said, "No one takes it from me, but I lay it down of my own accord. I have authority to lay it down and authority to take it up again. This command I received from my Father." John 10:18.

> "*God entered human suffering. God was in Jesus Christ, experiencing and tasting the agony of human suffering. God was in Jesus Christ, experiencing and tasting the agony of human suffering.*"

Christ had already confirmed all of the agony of the Cross, all of the pain of the Crown of thorns that was knocked on His head, as well as the nails in His hands and feet. It was offered freely. "I am thirsty" is the shortest phrase that Christ Jesus spoke on the Cross.

### The Cross and the Crucifixion

Believers must know that all of the agony, wounds, scourging, and stripes received from the beating, combined together on the Cross stand as thirst. God, on the Cross, laid out the mystery of incarnation. God entered human suffering. God was in Jesus Christ, experiencing and tasting the agony of human suffering.

> "*On the Cross, Christ showed us our own suffering and showed us that God knows our suffering. He identified with all of our earthly suffering.*"

Christ wanted to give us a new life by taking away the old life, the life in which we are always thirsty and hungry for worldly pleasures, the life of sin and death. He wanted to give us water so that we should never thirst again, just as He asked the Samaritan woman, "Will you give me a drink?" John 4:7.

On the Cross, Christ was thirsty because he gave living water. He offered us this on the Cross, just as He offered it to the woman at the well. He went through all we are going through on the Cross because He put Himself in our position. He humbled Himself on the Cross.

On the Cross, Christ showed us our own suffering and showed us that God knows our suffering. He identified with all of our earthly suffering. On the Cross, God the Father in Christ Jesus showed us our thirst and rejection of His water of life.

At the same time, He reflects back to us our own sense of loss by showing us what it takes for God to endure our rejection of His love for us.

On the Cross, God the Father met our suffering with the suffering of Jesus in such a way that Jesus cried out. By Him, our thirst was met and our spirits were revived.

The people of the world, especially believers, have a spiritual manifestation in their lives. At the Cross, when Jesus cried "I am thirsty," that thirst was the thirst of humans' suffering hearts and the thirst of Jesus the giver of life were joined together through the power of the Holy Spirit, which will come to and abide with believers forever.

> *"At the Cross, when Jesus cried "I am thirsty," that thirst was the thirst of humans' suffering hearts and the thirst of Jesus the giver of life were joined together through the power of the Holy Spirit."*

Our Lord said, "The thief comes only to steal and kill and destroy; I have come that they may have life, and have it to the full." John 10:10.

"A jar of wine vinegar was there, so they soaked a sponge in it, put the sponge on a stalk of the hyssop plant, and lifted it to Jesus' lips." John 19:29.

This is a significant event that many believers might overlook. John mentioned the use of the hyssop plan when Christ was hanging on the Cross, to remind us of when blood was sprinkled on the door posts and lintels on the first Passover.

"Take a bunch of hyssop, dip it into the blood in the basin and put some of the blood on the top and on both sides of the doorframe. None of you shall go out of the door of your house until morning." Exodus 12:22.

This was associated with purification and sacrifice in the tabernacle. Therefore, Christ was given a hyssop sponge for purification before He sacrificed Himself for the sins of the whole world. Jesus drank the vinegar with hyssop before His last breath on the Cross. Jesus' words,

"I am thirsty" should remind believers of His physical nature and His humanity. "They put gall in my food and gave me vinegar for my thirst." Psalm 69:21.

> "*Our Lord suffered at the hands of the High Priest and Pilate for His righteousness, in order to make us righteous for God.*"

The psalmist bore rejection, shame, and alienation because of his righteous deed for God and for God's kingdom. He spoke against sin and pleaded for revival, cleansing, and reformation among God's people. For this, he suffered at the hands of the wicked, just as our Lord suffered at the hands of the High Priest and Pilate for His righteousness, in order to make us righteous for God.

> "*Christ's tasting of the vinegar was a fulfillment of the Old Testament prophecy.*"

The expression of the suffering of a righteous person captured the feelings of Christ as He went through torture and beatings from the Romans this shows a great deal of His experience and agony on the Cross. Christ's tasting of the vinegar was a fulfillment of the Old Testament prophecy. It was the flesh or humanity of Jesus that was thirsty. His thirst was not for earthly water.

We have to remember that Jesus did not need His human thirst to be quenched, because Jesus created the ocean, walked on the ocean, and created the rivers, rain, and snow. He did not need earthly water because He is the water of life.

"But whoever drinks the water I give them will never thirst. Indeed, the water I give them will become in them a spring of water welling up to eternal life." John 4:14. Also Jesus said, "Then Jesus declared, 'I am the bread of life. Whoever comes to me will never go hungry, and whoever believes in me will never be thirsty.'" John 6:35. He did not need water. With His power, He could have called the rain to fall and quench His thirst.

> *"Christ was thirsty for man to be filled with the Spirit of God."*

Christ was thirsty to restore humanity's relationship with His Father. "So God created mankind in his own image, in the image of God he created them; male and female he created them." Gen 1:27.

Christ was thirsty for man to be filled with the Spirit of God, "But the Advocate, the Holy Spirit, whom the Father will send in my name, will teach you all things and will remind you of everything I have said to you." John 14:26.

> *"He told us that we should be thirsty for sinners and the lost. We should open our eyes for their physical and spiritual needs."*

Christ was thirsty, so that we would not be thirsty. Jesus Christ said, "I thirst." He wants people to receive what He has given. Christ is thirsty for souls to be saved. He is thirsty for the people that He came to save, for sinners, the lost, and unbelievers.

He told us that we should be thirsty for sinners and the lost. We should open our eyes for their physical and spiritual needs. We need to feed them with the message of salvation that will lead them to the gift of eternal life that Christ came to provide.

> "We need to feed others with the message of salvation that will lead them to the gift of eternal life that Christ came to provide."

Christ does not want us to be a silent Christians. We must speak the word of God to the world. He was thirsty for souls to come and drink. He was thirsty for believers to come and call others to see the goodness of the Lord.

Christ was thirsty for believers who have dedicated their hearts to the Gospel of God for saving the souls of others, reaching the ends of the world for them, bringing the good news to the people, teaching, and preaching the Gospel in any season, rain or shine, so that idol worshipers will forsake their idols and follow Christ, giving their lives to Christ completely and totally.

> "Christ was thirsty for those who would spread the word of God to the lost world."

Christ was thirsty for those who would spread the word of God to the lost world. Jesus Christ suffered. He said, "I am thirsty," on the Cross, so that He could be able to give us the water of life, so that we would never be thirsty any more for the water of life that bubbles with the eternal life that the Holy Spirit produces and supplies to those who give their lives to Christ.

> *"Christ was thirsty for those who would spread the word of God to the lost world."*

"Jesus answered her, 'If you knew the gift of God and who it is that asks you for a drink, you would have asked him and he would have given you living water.'" John 4:10.

In other Scriptures, our Lord said, "On the last and greatest day of the festival, Jesus stood and said in a loud voice, 'Let anyone who is thirsty come to me and drink. Whoever believes in me, as Scripture has said, rivers of living water will flow from within them.'" John 7:37-38.

# 9

# "It Is Finished."
## John 19:30

Jesus' words, "It is finished" are victorious words that mean that His work on earth or redemptive work has been completed. They could also mean, "complete in Christ." We are complete. There will be no more separation from God, no more fear, no more condemnation, and no more guilt.

> *"Believers are the living stones built upon the truth with which divine Spirit unites His people. They are Christ's living stones, built up into house of God."*

Our salvation was completed on the Cross. Believers are the living stones built upon the truth with which divine Spirit unites His people. They are Christ's living stones, built up into house of God. Believers are the temple of God. Christ is believers' hope of glory. We are one in Christ. Christ is our source of life.

The moment our Lord said "It is finished," He declared himself the sacrificial Lamb of God for us from earth to heaven. From then on, the proclamation of His Holy name has been heard.

The psalmist says: "They will proclaim his righteousness, declaring to a people yet unborn: He has done it!." Psalm 22:31.

"For Christ also suffered once for sins, the righteous for the unrighteous, to bring you to God. He was put to death in the body but made alive in the Spirit." 1 Peter 3:18.

> *"The message of the Cross is so important, significant, foundational, and powerful."*

The message of the Cross is so important, significant, foundational, and powerful that Paul said: "For no one can lay any foundation other than the one already laid, which is Jesus Christ." 1 Cor 3:11. "For many walk, of whom I have told you often, and now tell you even weeping, that they are the enemies of the Cross of Christ." Php 3:18.

"For I resolved to know nothing while I was with you except Jesus Christ and him crucified."1 Cor 2:2. "We were therefore buried with him through baptism into death in order that, just as Christ was raised from the dead through the glory of the Father, we too may live a new life." Rom 6:4.

Many churches seem not to preach the message of the Cross. They look for various kinds of motivational messages to inspire their congregations and any messages related to lifestyles that their congregations can admire. They focus on financial prosperity and relationships.

They have forgotten the basis why we are saved, which is the Cross of Christ, and the reason the Spirit of God descended upon the earth on the day of Pentecost. They completely do away with the forgiveness of sin, the resurrection of the body, and life everlasting through the finished work of Jesus Christ on the Cross.

> *"If the Church does not preach, teach, and proclaim the Cross of Christ, the people and the congregations will not get or receive the true message of salvation or be able to be fully complete in Christ."*

The main aspect and the truth of the Gospel is that, unless a believer embraces the Cross and crucifies him or herself as Christ was crucified, they will never be one in Christ or know the power of His resurrection and the power of indwelling of the Spirit of God.

If the church do not preach, teach, and proclaim the Cross of Christ, the people and the congregations will not get or receive the true message of salvation or be able to be fully complete in Christ.

It is finished! In Jesus, we see the Spirit of God manifest in the flesh, showing that mankind is one with God. Believers need to believe that it is finished. We need to look within ourselves for a good relationship with the Creator and worship Him in spirit and in truth.

> *"We need to have close heart-to-heart communion with our heavenly Father who is the divine spirit of all creation and of all human souls."*

We need to have close heart-to-heart communion with our heavenly Father who is the divine spirit of all creation and of all human souls. We must make the Cross central in our witnessing to the lost, unbelievers, and sinners.

Some people witness without mentioning the Cross. They present the appealing parts of the Gospel, alerting attention to whatever can make their hearers accept the Gospel.

They are not making disciples or witnessing the true Gospel to the people. "For I resolved to know nothing while I was with you except Jesus Christ and him crucified." 1 Cor 2:2. Paul said that his concentration and our concentration in preaching should not be based on human wisdom—whether earthly or from any church.

Instead, we must concentrate on the central truth of the Gospel of God, which is redemption through Christ, and on the power of the indwelling of the Holy Spirit. We must not rely on ourselves, but on the message of the Gospel, which will result in a greater demonstration of the Spirit's work and power in our lives.

> *"The enemies of the Cross are those who profess to be believers, but are corrupting the Gospel through their immoral lives and false teachings."*

The enemies of the Cross are those who profess to be believers, but are corrupting the Gospel through their immoral lives and false teachings. Paul was very sad because of the false teachers.

The same still goes on today in our society. Some churches preach false Gospels and have turned the Bible and the word of God upside down. They preach what they think and believe that people want to hear. Some of them leave the Cross totally out of the picture.

Some even tell their congregations that they should never wear the Cross on their neck, instructing that they should take the Cross off of their necks, and should not even put it anywhere in their homes.

"We were therefore buried with him through baptism into death in order that, just as Christ was raised from the dead through the glory of the Father, we too may live a new life." Rom 6:4.

We must be aware that water baptism for the believer represents his or her death, burial, and resurrection in Jesus Christ. If it is done with true faith, baptism stands for the believer's rejection of sin and commitment to Christ, which will result in the flowing of abundant grace and a spiritually divine life.

Baptism also represents the believer's identification with Christ in His death and burial, in order that we may live in union with His resurrected life.

> "*The life of sin of the believer has been put to death with Christ on the Cross, in order that the believer might receive a new life in Christ and become a new person.*"

Just as Christ raised those who truly believe and exercise true saving faith in Him from death, so they could walk in the newness of life, the believer's old self has been crucified with Christ on the Cross. The life of sin of the believer has been put to death with Christ on the Cross, in order that the believer might receive a new life in Christ and become a new person.

The body of sin has been crucified and died. This is the human body that is controlled by sinful desires.

From that moment on, the Spirit of God takes total control of the believer's body. The believer's body becomes the Temple of the Holy Spirit.

Christ said He finished the work that God had assigned Him to do, in His priestly prayer. John 17:4. Our Lord said, "It is finished," declaring that the work was done and that the results would continue. Not only was Jesus Christ's redemptive work and mission finished, but also, all who believe in Jesus Christ will continue to draw on the work accomplished on the Cross.

> *"Jesus Christ and God the Father will not add anything to the work it has been forever fulfilled, completed, and finished on the Cross."*

Jesus Christ and God the Father will not add anything to the work it has been forever fulfilled, completed, and finished on the Cross. We believers cannot add to it, it is finished. These were Christ's word to anyone who would say that believers' redemption needs some further work for victory over sin, death, Satan, or hell.

It was a shout of triumph and victory, declaring the work of redemption accomplished, on the Cross. "It is finished." Christ uttered his last final words with a loud voice, "It is finished." This cry signified the end of his suffering and the completion of the work of redemption.

## The Cross and the Crucifixion

The debt for our sins was paid in full and the plan of salvation established. The curtain separating the Holy place from the most Holy place barred the way to the presence of God. This means that a path was now open to the presence of God.

> *"He finished the entire work of redemption. The work of our salvation, our victory over sin and death, was accomplished."*

Through the death of Christ, the curtain was removed and the path to the most Holy place, God's presence, was opened for all who believe in Christ and His saving message. He finished the entire work of redemption. The work of our salvation, our victory over sin and death, was accomplished. He breathed His last breath and died on the Cross for you and me.

> *"When Jesus Christ said, 'It is finished,' that meant that everything the Father had assigned for Him to do had been done and completed."*

Christ crushed the head of Satan on the Cross, permanently. He set us free from humanity's bondage of lies and deceit imposed by Satan, just as the Father said in the Garden of Eden, when Adam and Eve fell because of Satan's deceit. When Jesus Christ said, "It is finished," that meant that everything the Father had assigned for Him to do had been done and completed, as well as His physical, earthly life, which had also been completed as written.

We have to remember that, in the Book of Psalms, Jesus said, "Then I said, 'Here I am, I have come—it is written about me in the scroll. I desire to do your will, my God; your law is within my heart.'" Psalm 40:7-8.

> *"When our Lord said 'It is finished,' He was referring to the word of redemption that He had completed."*

Therefore, when our Lord said "It is finished," He was referring to the word of redemption that He had completed. Also, we have to remember what He said when He was twelve years old and was in the Temple.

He told His mother and His earthly father, "And he said unto them, 'how is it that ye sought me? Why were you searching for me?' he asked. 'Didn't you know I had to be in my Father's house?'" Luke 2:49.

> *"The words of Jesus on the Cross made it clear that He was the Messiah and that He had completed the task that had been assigned to Him."*

And on another occasion, He told His disciples: "'My food,' said Jesus, 'is to do the will of him who sent me and to finish his work.'" John 4:34. These words of Jesus on the Cross made it clear that He was the Messiah and that He had completed the task that had been assigned to Him.

All of the prophecies from the beginning of creation in the Old Testament were fulfilled through Christ. The suffering of the Messiah had been accomplished. When the Temple cloths from the Holy of Holies were ripped in two, from top to the bottom, this confirmed that the old order of the sacrificial, ceremonial law of goats and bulls had been canceled completely and forever.

> "*Christ will forever be our mediator of a new covenant, sitting at the right hand of God, asking and pleading our case to the Father on our behalf.*"

Christ, the sacrificial Lamb of God, offered Himself once and for all on the Cross. His atoning blood paid for our sin. The work of Jesus on earth, with His bodily form, ended, this also marked that He will forever be our mediator of a new covenant, sitting at the right hand of God, asking and pleading our case to the Father on our behalf.

Before His crucifixion, in His priestly prayer, He glorified the Father. He confirmed that He had finished the work that the Father had given Him to do: "I have brought you glory on earth by finishing the work you gave me to do." John 17:4.

> "*It is finished. Christ's suffering work on earth was done.*"

It is finished. Christ's suffering work on earth was done. We have to remember how hard He prayed in the garden of Gethsemane, with sweat of blood, but told the Father that His Father's will, would be done, not His will.

# 10

# "Father, Into Your Hands I Commit My Spirit."
### Luke 23:46

Christ said, "Father, into your hands I commit my Spirit." These were Jesus' last words before His death. Faithful believers, in their dying hours, have often used these words.

These words show dependence on God and faith in His goodness to His people.

> "*Believers must commit themselves to God's care, not only during danger, trouble, and difficulties, but also throughout the positive events in their lives.*"

Believers must commit themselves to God's care. It is a very important and appropriate thing to do, not only during danger, trouble, and difficulties, but also throughout the positive events in their lives.

We should learn from the Scripture that our Lord quoted while on the Cross. It showed that He knew the Scripture and, at that moment, Christ used the Scripture to preach to His people. This is very important for understanding that Jesus Christ loved His people and wanted to reach out to them and touch them with His love and compassion.

> *"Christ gave up His Spirit for you and me. Christ sacrificed His life as the Passover lamb for us."*

He wanted them to believe in Him, at that moment on the Cross, and He is still reaching out to them today. Christ gave up His Spirit for you and me. Christ sacrificed His life as the Passover lamb for us.

From the Cross, Jesus confidently proclaimed this truth. He spoke with a loud voice, in the middle of His suffering and death. The Creator of life gave up His life, His perfect life, and He gave in to death, with perfect faith in His Father's hands.

Christ's words on the Cross are words of great and pure comfort to all of His people, both at that time as well as to those of us who believe in Him today. His words teach and encourage us to trust him and to be united with Him in His death, burial, and resurrection.

Christ's words become our words because He fills us with Himself. We should follow His footsteps and

## The Cross and the Crucifixion

trust Him as He trusted the Father. The faith of Jesus Christ on the Cross becomes our faith. His strength becomes our strength. Christ's Cross speaks to us today, confidently, clearly, and loudly, just as He cried with a loud voice on the Cross, "Father, into your hands I commit my Spirit."

As we are in Christ, we should commit our spirit, soul, and body into His hands. Just as He committed Himself into the hands of the Father, so, too, He committed those of us who believe in Him into the Father's hands—before the beginning of creation and until He returns to this earth.

> *"Believers must commit their lives, problems, difficulties, adversities, pains, and illness, even at the time of death, into the hands of the one who is one with them."*

Believers must commit their lives, problems, difficulties, adversities, pains, and illness, even at the time of death, into the hands of the one who is one with them, just as He and Father are one.

From the Cross, Jesus boldly and confidently proclaimed the truth with a clear and loud voice, "Father into your hands I commit my spirit." He laid down His life for our transgressions.

He gave us His life that we might have life, life everlasting. This is the source of believers' confidence and rejoicing that Christ came to this world to save sinners and to reconcile us with God the Father.

All believers in Jesus Christ are committed into the Father's hands by Christ. The Father sees us in Christ. All of our sins have been forgiven and we are washed clean with the blood of the Lamb of God who took away the sin of the whole world.

> *"Believers must proclaim His Holy name. He is worthy of all of our thankfulness and praises."*

All believers must praise and glorify the Lord Jesus Christ today and forever and hear His words on the Cross where He was crucified for you and me. Believers must proclaim His Holy name. He is worthy of all of our thankfulness and praises.

We must look at Jesus on the Cross, unite with Him on the Cross, live our lives for Him, look at our past, present, and future lives, and look at our lives with him in His kingdom, where we will spend eternity with Him in a new earth where righteousness will rule.

On the Cross is where God the Father Almighty, God the Son, and God the Holy Spirit demonstrate His magnificent love for us. It is where Christ our

*The Cross and the Crucifixion*

Savior accomplished His redemptive work for humanity. At the Cross, our souls find salvation, satisfaction, love, joy, happiness, the gift of grace, and heaven and the inheritance that is in it.

"Father, into your hands I commit my spirit"—these words of our Lord on the Cross show an act of contentment, trust, confidence, faith, and love. Christ knows and trusts the Father.

*"There is no love like the love of a Father, and our Father in heaven is worthy of our trust, our faith, and our confidence."*

There is no love like the love of a Father, and our Father in heaven is worthy of our trust, our faith, and our confidence. He is worthy for us to commit our spirits into His holy hands.

As His sons and daughters, the children of God, Christ wants us to commit our spirits, souls, and bodies into the hands of the Father, who is the giver of lives. Christ's life is our lives.

If Christ committed His spirit into the Father's hands, we should do the same in order to have life through the Spirit of the living God, which is an amazing and incomprehensible experience. The human spirit is the highest of all beings.

This spirit distinguishes man from the beasts or animals. This spirit connects human beings to God.

This spirit is formed within us. Prophet Zechariah said, "A prophecy: The word of the LORD concerning Israel. The LORD, who stretches out the heavens, who lays the foundation of the earth, and who forms the human spirit within a person." Zech 12:1.

> *"Jesus Christ gave His spirit into the hands of the Father through faith."*

"And the dust returns to the ground it came from, and the spirit returns to God who gave it." Ecc 12:7. This special verse distinguishes between the aspect of human person that remains at the time of death and the aspect that returns to God. Jesus Christ gave His spirit into the hands of the Father through faith.

Christ spoke in a loud voice, with all of His strength and power, because He wanted everyone to hear Him. For twelve hours, Jesus was in the hands of men, as he had told His disciples before the day of crucifixion.

"When they came together in Galilee, he said to them, "The Son of Man is going to be delivered into the hands of men." Matt 17:22.

> *"Christ delivered Himself into the hands of sinners voluntarily. He delivered His spirit into the hands of the Father."*

## The Cross and the Crucifixion

Christ submitted Himself as a lamb to the slaughter when the time of His crucifixion finally arrived. Christ delivered Himself into the hands of sinners voluntarily.

He delivered His spirit into the hands of the Father. His spirit will be completely and forever in the hands of His Father because Christ and the Father are one from the beginning of creation.

God the Father, God the Son, and God the Holy Spirit are one. He is forever out of the hands of men. Never again will He be in the hands of the wicked and never again will He suffer shame or pain.

*"The Father exalted Jesus high above all the principalities and powers in all of creation and in every name that was named, and set Him at His right hand in the heavens."*

Jesus offered Himself as atonement for our sins, once and for all, as a sacrificial Lamb of God. He gave His spirit into the hands of his Father. Three days after his crucifixion, the Father raised Him from the dead.

After forty days, when He permanently ascended into heaven, the Father exalted Him high above all the principalities and powers in all of creation and in every name that was named, and set Him at His right hand in the heavens. He is seated at the right hand of the

Father's throne, waiting until all His enemies are made His foot stool.

Christ came back into communion with the Father because the communion was not broken when He carried the sin of the whole world on the Cross, as the light of God the Father was hidden from Him during that time.

> *"The Father will send His son back to power and great glory, so that He may rule and reign over all the nations of the whole earth with iron hands. He shall judge them in truth and in righteousness."*

On the Cross, Christ never broke His union with His Father. There was a perfect union because the Father is the one who gave Christ the cup full of the sins of the whole world to Him to drink, and Christ accepted the cup of wrath from the Father's hands.

According to the Bible, the Father will send His son back to power and great glory, so that He may rule and reign over all the nations of the whole earth with iron hands. He shall judge them in truth and in righteousness.

Christ was on the Cross for the sins of all of humanity. He was our representative on the Cross. Christ took away all of humanity's sins and bore them on the Cross. Christ is our sin bearer.

## The Cross and the Crucifixion

The Father saw Him on the Cross as our and, as if He were seeing the sins of all of the people in the whole world, He put His wrath on His Son who was our sin bearer on the Cross.

When the Lord Jesus said that He committed His spirit to the Father, He automatically committed the spirits of all people who believe in the Gospel and surrender their lives to His Lordship. God the Father accepted Christ's spirit as well as our spirits.

> "*Christ clothes us with His righteousness and holiness. We are forever children of God, just as Christ is the Son of God.*"

Christ came to this world, lived in this world, was crucified, died, was buried, and rose to life again because of sinners, which means you and me. He went through all of the agony of the Cross and crucifixion because of you and me and all believers.

Christ gathered the souls of the entire human race and presented them to God the Father. From that moment on, God the Father has seen those who are in Christ as Christ. When God sees us in Christ, our past, present, and future sins are forgiven.

Christ clothes us with His righteousness and holiness. We are forever children of God, just as Christ is the Son of God. "My Father, who has given them to me, is greater than all; no one can snatch them out of my Father's hand." John 10:29.

All believers in Jesus Christ are born with the Spirit of God. Our Lord told Nicodemus, "Who through faith are shielded by God's power until the coming of the salvation that is ready to be revealed in the last time." 1 Peter 1:5.

All the saints of God are born of His spirit. The spirit of the all-knowing, all-powerful, all-merciful, and gracious, loving God.

The spirit is given to all believers through Jesus Christ, our Redeemer King. Throughout the time that the sovereign Savior spent on the Cross in great suffering and agony, He was in communion and good fellowship with the Father.

> *"In any circumstances, difficulties, afflictions, persecutions, and adversities, we must call on our Lord and Savior who is seated at the right hand of His Father's throne, interceding for us."*

All believers should follow this great truth: in whatever conditions we may be, we must continue with our personal relationship, fellowship, and communion with our heavenly Father and with Jesus Christ, the author and finisher of our faith.

In any circumstances, difficulties, afflictions, persecutions, and adversities, we must call on our Lord and Savior who is seated at the right hand of His Father's throne, interceding for us.

Communion is a very important aspect of our faith in the Lord. Christ communicated with the Father on the Cross, even though He was in great agony. He prayed and spoke seven times. Communion strengthens our faith in times of troubles and tribulations.

Communion sheds a great light on our problems that no one else can solve. Communion helps us focus on the love of God during times when our hearts want to tremble because of earthly problems.

> "Christ Jesus has the power and infinite love to relieve us from all of our pain if we rest on Him."

Believers must be able to see clearly that when Christ said, "Into your hands, I commit my Spirit," and rested his head with the crown of thorns on it, His Father's hand was under His head to relieve Him from agony and pain at that time.

He has the power and infinite love to relieve us from all of our pain if we rest on Him. The power to be like Jesus was passed through His unfailing love on the Cross. He was lifted up in glory on the Cross during His crucifixion, which enabled Him to impart His spirit in us.

## The Cross and the Crucifixion

Jesus willingly gave up His life on the Cross by committing His spirit to God. His life was not taken away from him. Christ gave His life for us sinners on the Cross.

The centurion who was there at that time, when He saw that Jesus had died, believed that Christ truly was the Son of God. His seven last words began with Father and ended with Father.

This shows us the intimacy between the Father and the Son. In the Garden of Gethsemane, He called on His Father. "Father, if you are willing, take this cup from me; yet not my will, but yours be done." Luke 22:42.

Our Lord called on the Father three times in the Garden of Gethsemane. "Father" was His first word on the Cross and "Father" was His last word on the Cross.

> *"Jesus Christ wants us to live a life of dependence on Him in any circumstances of life."*

Jesus demonstrated the Fatherhood of God. Our Lord demonstrated His love and dependence on the Father for everything. This shows all believers how we must strengthen our relationship with Christ, God the Father, and the Holy Spirit. Jesus Christ wants us to live a life of dependence on Him in any circumstances of life.

> *"Jesus wants us to focus and put everything in His hands, just as He focused and called on the Father in everything that He was going through on earth."*

Jesus wants us to focus and put everything in His hands, just as He focused and called on the Father in everything that He was going through on earth, up until His last hour on the Cross.

God's hands are connected to the hands of the angels. God performs all of his activities and actions through the hands of the angels and all of the heavenly hosts.

Jesus Christ was sustained by angelic hands on the Cross, which fulfilled the Messianic prophecy: "But his bow remained steady, his strong arms stayed limber, because of the hand of the Mighty One of Jacob, because of the Shepherd, the Rock of Israel." Gen 49:24.

Throughout the Scriptures, God's hands are revealed in His work of creation. Christ died for our sins, according to the Scriptures. Moses and Elijah spoke of the Cross, which He would accomplish by Himself. The breaking of the bread at the last supper demonstrated that Christ gave His body for sinners.

The drinking of wine at the last supper indicated that Christ shed His blood for sinners on the Cross. Christ's death was an act of obedience to God the Father's command to die on the Cross.

The death of Christ was a demonstration of a greater love for His friends. Christ is the true friend of sinners.

> *"Christ poured out His soul in death in order to redeem sinners. The death of Christ was a demonstration of a greater love for His friends. Christ is the true friend of sinners."*

Our Lord said, "Just as the Father knows me and I know the Father—and I lay down my life for the sheep. I have other sheep that are not of this sheep pen. I must bring them also. They too will listen to my voice, and there shall be one flock and one shepherd.

The reason my Father loves me is that I lay down my life—only to take it up again. No one takes it from me, but I lay it down of my own accord. I have authority to lay it down and authority to take it up again. This command I received from my Father." John 10:15-18.

Therefore, the death of Christ was an act of giving. It was an act of sacrifice beyond limits and beyond comprehension. No one took Christ's life from Him. He laid it down by Himself. He laid it down for us sinners. "Walk in the way of love, just as Christ loved us and gave himself up for us as a fragrant offering and sacrifice to God." Eph 5:2.

> *"Believers must be full of praises and thankfulness, to such an extent that they will not have room in their hearts for any form of sin or sinful nature."*

Paul told us to walk in love and to love each other, as Christ loved us and gave His life for us. Believers must be full of praises and thankfulness, to such an extent that they will not have room in their hearts for any form of sin or sinful nature.

We will trust in Christ at all times and not fulfill the lust of the flesh. We will be able to appreciate what Christ has done for us on the Cross by laying down His life for our sins.

We will be filled with Jesus' life and, therefore, we will be able to live lives of true love and devotion for one another. We will be able to live the lives that the Lord Jesus Christ wants us to live for His glory.

Christ laid down His life for us on the Cross, so that "He saved us, not because of righteous things we had done, but because of his mercy. He saved us through the washing of rebirth and renewal by the Holy Spirit." Titus 3:5.

## The Cross and the Crucifixion

The Father loved the Son because He laid down His life before the creation of the universe. Here, we see the love within the soul of the Almighty Father towards His Son on the Cross.

Our Lord saw His death on the Cross as a baptism for which He was ready. "But I have a baptism to undergo, and what constraint I am under until it is completed!" Luke 12:50. Christ spoke about the baptism to which He was called. He saw it as His prophetic suffering, His crucifixion, and His death.

> *"Bread symbolizes the gift of His sacrifice as the bread of life—the bread that came or was coming down from heaven throughout His earthly life."*

Jesus spoke about manna that comes down from heaven as one of the symbols of His body, which He gave on the Cross. Bread symbolizes the gift of His sacrifice as the bread of life—the bread that came or was coming down from heaven throughout His earthly life.

"But here is the bread that comes down from heaven, which anyone may eat and not die. I am the living bread that came down from heaven. Whoever eats this bread will live forever. This bread is my flesh, which I will give for the life of the world." John 6:50-51.

# 11

# The Significance of the Number Seven from Creation

The number seven represents fullness. It is also a favored number in the Bible. Our Lord said we must forgive seventy times seven times, which represents the fullness of the forgiveness of God.

"Then Peter came to Jesus and asked, 'Lord, how many times shall I forgive my brother or sister who sins against me? Up to seven times?' Jesus answered, 'I tell you, not seven times, but seventy-seven times'" Matt 18:21-22.

God created the heavens and the earth in seven days, and He called everything He created very well. On the seventh day, the Bible tells us that God blessed the seventh day because that was the day that the Lord God rested after having carried out the work of creation. God created the universe in seven days, marking the fullness of time.

## The Cross and the Crucifixion

Our Lord spoke seven times from the Cross and this is significant because seven, in the Bible, is the number of completion or perfection. His first word was a prayer of forgiveness for the people who crucified Him and for us today, because we are all sinners and we do not know what we are doing.

We still crucify Christ today and put Him to shame, because some people in this world do not want God in their lives, kicking God out of everything they are doing and out of their lives.

> "*Christ's prayer of forgiveness still continues with us today because He does not want anyone to perish.*"

Christ's prayer of forgiveness still continues with us today because He does not want anyone to perish. He wants everyone to gain knowledge of repentance and to pray for the forgiveness that is only in Him.

Christ's second word was an answer to the thief who was nailed on the Cross next to Him and asked for salvation by faith. He responded to the thief's demand, because the thief put His faith in Him, knowing that Christ was the only one who could save him. He believed that Christ was the true Son of God, according to his observations beside the Cross of Christ.

The thief believed that Christ was the Lord and God and that He was the true Son of God. He spread the forgiveness of His prayer to the thief and gave him eternal life. This particular thief was the first sinner in the history of the work of redemption who received forgiveness of his sins and the gift of grace through the saving faith of salvation and eternal life. His third word constituted words of love to the people He loved who were at the foot of the Cross.

The blood of Christ made atonement for human souls. Christ spoke seven times on the Cross. Therefore, the number seven means perfection, as well as joy and rest. At the same time, our Lord Jesus Christ, when He was on the Cross where the work of redemption was completed, spoke to us seven times.

His first word on the Cross was a word of prayer. He prayed for those who were crucifying Him, for sinners, and for the lost. He prayed for those who believe in Him through the work of redemption.

> *"Christ prayed that prayer of forgiveness again and again, and He continues to pray the same prayer for us today so that we may live in him through the power of the Holy Spirit."*

Christ prayed that prayer of forgiveness again and again, and He continues to pray the same prayer for us today so that we may live in him through the power of the Holy Spirit.

The third word was for His mother. Just as our Lord wanted John to substitute Him in caring for His mother, in the same way, our Lord wants us to substitute Him in reaching for the sinners and the lost whom He came to save. Jesus came to die for the sins of all people in the world—the living as well as those who have yet to be born.

Christ is the Lord and God of all people in the world. The fourth word was when Christ cried, in a loud voice, "My God My God why have you forsaken me?" At that time, Christ had been separated from the Father of lights. God turned His back on his Son.

> *"Just as God separated Himself from Adam and Even when they fell into sin, the same God separated Himself from His Son, because He took the sins of the whole world on Him in order to save us."*

It was the first time that this had happened to Jesus. Just as God separated Himself from Adam and Even when they fell into sin, the same God separated Himself from His Son, because He took the sins of the whole world on Him in order to save us.

The fifth word that our Lord spoke on the Cross was "I am thirsty." Christ was thirsty for all human souls, from then, until His return to judge the quick and the dead.

The sixth word that Christ spoke on the Cross was "It is finished." Christ told us that the work for which He left His glory in heaven, put on our humanity, became like us, and lived with us for thirty-three years was finished, completed, and accomplished. He shed His precious blood for you and me. Christ paid it all with His blood on the Cross.

The seventh word that Christ spoke on the Cross was, "Father into your hands, I commit my Spirit." This was a word of trust from Christ to God the Father, and it was a word of love and contentment.

> *"All believers must pray in order to be able to live in the power of the Holy Spirit."*

This was the last prayer from the Lord to the Father. Christ always prayed to the Father, to the point that the apostles admired His prayers so much that they asked Him to teach them how to pray.

All believers must pray in order to be able to live in the power of the Holy Spirit. Christ also teaches us the importance of prayer and the parable of the unjust judge.

Christ told us to pray without season, asking, knocking, receiving, and seeking in our prayers to help us to increase our trust and faith in Him. We should pray for assurance, our Lord said. We must believe that we will receive and shall have everything we ask for and desire in prayer.

As believers, we must always remember what our Lord has done for us in the past, what He is doing for us now, and what He is going to continue doing for us in the years to come.

We must also give thanks to our heavenly Father for His protection, guidance, and provisions, during our troubles, adversities, tribulations, afflictions, and pains. He is always there for us, comforting us through the power of His Spirit.

> "*Christ Jesus is the God of infinite love, the God of infinite mercy, the God of grace, the God of salvation, the God of great compassion, the God of justice, and a Holy God.*"

We are all children of God, through our faith in Jesus Christ, the Redeemer King. Christ Jesus is the God of infinite love, the God of infinite mercy, the God of grace, the God of salvation, the God of great compassion, the God of justice, and a Holy God. On the Cross, infinite justice is satisfied and love is perfected.

At the age of twelve years old, He told His mother and Father in Jerusalem that He must do His Father's business. He told the Scribes and the Pharisees, "As the Father does so I do. I do not do anything on my own.

I do as the Father does. The Father does all the work through me." He said, "I am the vine; my Father is the Gardener."

He said to Philip, "If you have seen me, you have seen the Father. I do not do the work alone; the Father does all the work through me." He also said, "As the Father loved me, so I have loved you continue ye in my love."

He said, "I will ask the Father, He will send the Holy Spirit in my name." John 14, 15, and 17.

> *"Believers must imitate Christ and let Christ's will be our will, let Christ's love be our love, and do everything with Christ's love, strength, and power."*

His seventh word on the Cross, which was His last word, was, "Father, into your hands I commit my Spirit." After the resurrection, on the day of ascension, His last word on earth was "As the Father sent me, so I have sent you; go and preach the salvation to all the people."

He mentions His father in His great priestly prayer in the Book of John, chapter 17. His will was His Father's will. His desire was His Father's desire. Christ's time was the Father's time, Christ strength was His Father's strength and Christ's love was His Father's love. Christ's will was to do His Father's work and complete it.

## The Cross and the Crucifixion

Christ came to do His Father's will, not His own will. Christ said, "I and my Father are one." Believers must imitate Christ and let Christ's will be our will, let Christ's love be our love, and do everything with Christ's love, strength, and power.

> *"Jesus wants us to know that no one can pluck us out of His Father's hands. The Holy hands of the Father support us from this earth to eternity."*

Jesus wants us to know that no one can pluck us out of His Father's hands. The Holy hands of the Father support us from this earth to eternity. We have been sealed with the power of the indwelling of the Holy Spirit forever.

The seal of the Holy Spirit cannot be broken. We are well secured in the holy hands of God. Christ wants sinners to repent, so that they can be sealed and empowered by the Spirit of God, whereby they will commit their spirits into the hands of God, from this earth to heaven.

At the Cross, there were seven churches. "I will strike her children dead. Then all the churches will know that I am he who searches hearts and minds, and I will repay each of you according to your deeds." Rev 2:23.

"Jesus called out with a loud voice, "Father, into your hands I commit my spirit." When he had said this, he breathed his last." Luke 23:46. Jesus voluntarily gave his life over to death. At that moment, He went, through the Spirit, to His father in heaven. The suffering of Christ came to an end.

The Cross of Christ symbolizes peace and demonstrates the power of God to save all of humanity. The Cross is where God the Father completed all of the work of reconciliation. The Cross is where Christ paid for our sins with His precious blood. Moreover, by His stripes, we are healed.

> *"The Cross is where Christ paid for our sins with His precious blood. Moreover, by His stripes, we are healed."*

"For he himself is our peace, who has made the two groups one and has destroyed the barrier, the dividing wall of hostility, by setting aside in his flesh the law with its commands and regulations." Eph 2:14-15.

The Cross showed up on 9/11 during the terrorist attacks. It is a symbol of Jesus Christ that lets us know that He is with us during afflictions, disasters, terrorist attacks, and any other forms of destruction that we might be go through on earth. The Cross stood right there, in the middle of the rubble at the World Trade Center.

It is a sign that lets us know that Jesus Christ is with us in times of suffering and times of the loss of our loved ones. The Cross stood on that day as our hope of eternal peace that can only come from the Prince of Peace. It shows that He is coming back to establish peace on earth forever.

The Cross stood to let us know that all of our loved ones who died in the 9/11 terrorist attacks gained the blessings of eternal rest, that they will not die anymore, and that they will forever live with Christ in heaven where there is no violence or nuclear power disasters.

> *"The appearance of the Cross is a symbol of comfort, hope, and mercy through which God is saying, 'You are not alone. I am with you in whatever you are going through. I have been there. I suffered for the sins of the whole world.'"*

Looking at the Cross during disasters brings about unspeakable healing and unimaginable joy to people seeing and looking at the Cross. The appearance of the Cross is a symbol of comfort, hope, and mercy through which God is saying, "You are not alone. I am with you in whatever you are going through. I have been there. I suffered for the sins of the whole world."

He carried our past, present, and future sins on the Cross so that we may live, worship, and praise Him from this earth to heaven. Also, seeing the Cross during a disaster is a sign of the promise of eternal life. In the Lord, there is no sorrow, no darkness, no hatred, and no discrimination against any race or color.

The Cross stood unshakable during the earthquake in Haiti where over 200,000 people died. The entire church turned into rubble, but the Cross in front of the church stood unshakable.

> *"Christ gave a sign to the people that he was with them and that he would never leave them or forsake them."*

Christ gave a sign to the people that he was with them and that he would never leave them or forsake them. It is a symbol telling them to pray more and more during any difficult time.

As the Cross of Christ stood in the middle of the rubble, we have to know or remember that Christ is the answer to all earthly problems, disasters, evils, violence, earthly natural disasters such as hurricanes, volcanoes, earthquakes, tsunamis, floods, and wildfires that continuously destroy homes, properties, land, and food crops, and all other earthly disasters.

The holy Bible says, "Do not worry about those who kill the body but they cannot kill the soul." He was crucified, dead, buried, and raised to life again, so that we could have life in Him life everlasting. The truth of the Gospel is that Christ is with us and God is for us.

## The Cross and the Crucifixion

The gospel of Jesus Christ is the Gospel of love, "For God so loved the world that he gave his one and only Son, that whoever believes in him shall not perish but have eternal life." John 3:16.

> *"The gospel of Jesus Christ is the Gospel of love."*

The reality of the war of terrorism is that it constituted a brutal crime against humanity. People are still mourning for their loved ones. The Cross at 9/11 was relocated, but many people still look at it and take a deep breath and smile.

The Cross builds hope, not just for Christians, but also for American Muslims, Jews, and all other people of religious faiths in the nation and in the world.

The prayer before the Cross of the Catholic Church in Haiti still stands after the earthquake. The location of Haiti's Cross in Port-au-Prince was like a graveyard with bodies of people everywhere. In the middle of this tragic earthquake, the Cross of Christ remained amidst the rubble.

It is a sign that the people of Haiti are in need of help that no human can offer; they are in need of God, because the Lord said, "Call onto me I shall answer thee." The people are in need of prayer—prayer that will heal their land, from bottom to top.

## The Cross and the Crucifixion

They need prayer to heal their suffering and to comfort those who are in mourning. They need prayer to call on God to renew their land and bring peace to their people.

Looking at the Cross, they will see God's sovereignty and God's goodness joining together at the Cross, relating to the suffering of Christ on the day of His crucifixion.

He was whipped and crucified the Lamb of God that took away the sins of the whole world. The Cross is a sign of rejoicing and makes people put their faith in God and thank Him that they are still alive. Where there is life, there is hope.

> *"The image of the Cross standing in the middle of the rubble is a symbol of God's love, and it also tells people that they should love each other."*

Looking at those who died, those who are alive must know that God kept them alive for a reason and for a purpose. Therefore, the image of the Cross standing in the middle of the rubble is a symbol of God's love, and it also tells people that they should love each other, especially those who survived the earthquake. All the people in the nation should worship God and live a new life of love for one another.

# 12

# The Meaning of the Cross as Found in God's Purpose

The meaning of the Cross as found in God's purpose: God announced it in the words of Isaiah seven hundred years before its fulfillment. God saw that it was the only solution for the sin of every human being in the world.

> *"Christ paid it all. He purchased us with His precious blood on the Cross. God's infinite love is manifest in the world."*

It was very painful for the Father and the Holy Spirit, but that is where the way of redemption for sinful man came from. God's justice conquered the sins of the whole world through our Lord Jesus Christ on the Cross on the day of His crucifixion. God offered His mercy and grace to sinners.

## The Cross and the Crucifixion

The Cross signifies the possibility of the salvation of all of the people in the world. It clears all of the misunderstandings and contradictions that we go through on earth. Christ paid it all. He purchased us with His precious blood on the Cross. God's infinite love is manifest in the world.

> "*Christ paid it all. He purchased us with His precious blood on the Cross. God's infinite love is manifest in the world.*"

Our Lord said, "I and my Father are one." John 10:30. Therefore, if Jesus and the Father are one, it means that when Christ was on the Cross, the Father was there with Him. When He was crucified, the Father was crucified with Him.

He and the Father made atonement for the sins of the whole world on the Cross. He gave His life voluntarily because of the sins of the world, through the Father's command. He and the Father accomplished the work of redemption on the Cross.

Both of them suffered for the sins of the world. The Son bore the sins. The Father condemned the sin of the world on the Cross. The Lord said they would never perish because of the power of the Cross and the salvation of Jesus Christ, through the Cross, on the Calvary.

The work of redemption was accomplished on the Cross. What God the Father planned, the Son carried out. He and the Father are one. The Spirit of God makes and produces the fruit of the Spirit in order for us to live, our lives of God. We are in His hands which means that we are in both the Father and the Son's hands.

> *"Christ said that He would not lose any of the believers that the Father gave to Him."*

The Father made us alive in Jesus and gave us Jesus' salvation. God gave Himself to us. Jesus said that all of the people that the Father gave to Him would come to Him. Christ said that He would not lose any of the believers that the Father gave to Him.

"Then Jesus declared, 'I am the bread of life. Whoever comes to me will never go hungry, and whoever believes in me will never be thirsty . . . ' For my Father's will is that everyone who looks to the Son and believes in him shall have eternal life, and I will raise them up at the last day." John 6:35, 40.

Christ is the Father's glory. We believers are the gift that the Father gave to the Son. The gift of salvation is so supernatural and incomprehensible that believers must rejoice in the Lord for what He has done.

The Father's love is so unique and so profound that we must rejoice. Our Lord is worthy of all praises for the purchase of redemption through His blood for all humanity, all the people in the world.

> "Christ's purchase of redemption never fails. On the Cross, Christ purchased our redemption. Jesus' purchase of our redemption is forever."

Christ's purchase of redemption never fails. On the Cross, Christ purchased our redemption. Jesus' purchase of our redemption is forever. No one can change or take us out of the Father and Himself. The love of the Holy Spirit is one.

This is God's plan and love. "I give them eternal life, and they shall never perish. No one will snatch them out of my hand. My Father, who has given them to me, is greater than all; no one can snatch them out of my Father's hand." John 10:28-29.

In this verse, our Lord Jesus made a precious promise to all who are Christ's sheep and all who put their faith in Christ.

This is the blessed assurance from the Lord: that they will never be sent away from God's love or from His presence, nor will any power or circumstance in all creation on earth take them from the Shepherd. God has secured their safety and their security, even for the sheep that are very weak or the weakest, but that follow and listen to the Shepherd that God has provided.

Christ said, "I am the bread of life." This was the first of seven 'I am' statements recorded in John's Gospel, each one emphasizing an important aspect of the personal ministry of Jesus.

This statement of Jesus tells us that He is the sustenance that nourishes spiritual life. The other "I am" statements were: "I am the good shepherd," "I am the resurrection and the life," "I am the way and the truth and the life," and "I am the true friend."

> "*Those who suffer because of their personal relationship with the Lord will be blessed because the Holy Spirit's presence and God's favor will rest on them in a special way, foreshadowing heaven's glory.*"

It is very important that every believer of Jesus Christ understand the relationship of the Father's will to human responsibility. It is not in the will of God that anyone should fall from grace and subsequently be separated from God. Neither, is it his will that any individual should perish or fail to come into knowledge of the truth and be saved.

*The Cross and the Crucifixion*

It is a principle within God's kingdom that suffering for Christ's sake will cause an increase in the believer's joy in the Lord. Those who suffer because of their personal relationship with the Lord will be blessed because the Holy Spirit's presence and God's favor will rest on them in a special way, foreshadowing heaven's glory.

Jesus is the light of the world. He is the true light. He removes darkness and deception by illuminating the right way to God and salvation.

> *"The saints will see Him face-to-face in His light, as the light of the world that took away the sin of the whole world."*

All believers in Jesus Christ are delivered from the power of darkness. Jesus is the gate. Those who enter through Him will be saved and will have abundant eternal lives. They will have all that they need to be delivered from sin and death. He will change our image to His glory—what a transformation that will be!

With His infinite touch and cleansing from sin, we will be as bright as the sun and these blessings will flow from our exalted Lamb of God, Jesus Christ. He will continue to be the center and the soul of eternal salvation for all those who believe in Him. The saints will see Him face-to-face in His light, as the light of the world that took away the sin of the whole world.

"Dear friends, now we are children of God, and what we will be has not yet been made known. But we know that when Christ appears, we shall be like him, for we shall see him as he is." 1 John 3:2.

> "*How blessed it is that His Father is our Father because of the Cross. It is unspeakable and very precious that we can call on a great and very alive God, our Father.*"

We are the children of God. What a glorious truth! Apostle Paul said, "It is because of him that you are in Christ Jesus, who has become for us wisdom from God—that is, our righteousness, holiness and redemption." 1 Cor 1:30.

"But if Christ is in you, then even though your body is subject to death because of sin, the Spirit gives life because of righteousness." Rom 8:10. This is a truth that surpasses knowledge and human comprehension.

How blessed it is that His Father is our Father because of the Cross. It is unspeakable and very precious that we can call on a great and very alive God, our Father. What comfort, what a blessed assurance that Jesus and the Father shed their love upon ordinary sinners.

God is our Father in heaven and He cares for all of His children. He provides for all of our needs according to His riches in glory. "But my God shall supply all your need according to his riches in glory by Christ Jesus." Php 4:19. God our Father protects and guides us. He will not allow any evil to befall His children.

> "*Jesus loved us, cleansed us with His precious blood, purchased us, put robes on us, made us His own forever, and, most importantly, He glorified us.*"

"In heaven" means that Jesus Christ chose us before the foundation of the world. He loved us, cleansed us with His precious blood, purchased us, put robes on us, made us His own forever, and, most importantly, He glorified us.

Therefore, the saints rejoice in the Lord Jesus Christ. "Light" also means beauty. Beauty always shows in darkness. Therefore, all of the beauty of the saints comes from Christ. Those who are in heaven are in the light of righteousness.

"But for you who revere my name, the sun of righteousness will rise with healing in its rays. And you will go out and frolic like well-fed calves." Mal 4:2. All saints have their lives being under the sun of righteousness.

Light also symbolizes knowledge. All of the mysteries of God and of heaven will be understood and clear, and all that causes confusion in our hearts will be plain to us because we will be in the light of the Lamb. We will offer praises and admiration to Him in heaven, with God's timeless love.

Light is also a revelation, because light reveals what is hidden. The world can never know what is in heaven, but with Christ's love, He receives us into heaven with all of the other denominations that agree on the Cross of Christ.

"May I never boast except in the Cross of our Lord Jesus Christ, through which the world has been crucified to me, and I to the world." Gal 6:14. Apostle Paul gloried in the Cross of Christ and in the power of the Cross.

> *"This shows the love of God. Whatever we are, we owe it to the Cross. The Cross reconciled us. There is a glorious future because of the Cross. Come to the Cross and find salvation, rest, peace, joy, and the love of God."*

This shows the love of God. Whatever we are, we owe it to the Cross. The Cross reconciled us. There is a glorious future because of the Cross. Christ died on the Cross. Come to the Cross and find salvation, rest, peace, joy, and the love of God.

All Christians who have made the Cross their lives no longer cherish or love the world, with all of its accepted standards and with its opinions values, honors, and lifestyles. We are crucified with Christ, which means that we have crucified our entire beings to the world.

> *"There is no sharing in the salvation and glory of Christ's Cross without turning from all worldly pleasures that may draw our hearts and minds away from Christ and His closeness."*

There is no sharing in the salvation and glory of Christ's Cross without turning from all worldly pleasures that may draw our hearts and minds away from Christ and His closeness.

# The Cross and the Crucifixion

# An Excerpt from Elizabeth C. Clephane's 1872 Song

Beneath the Cross of Jesus, I fain would take my stand; the shadow of a mighty Rock within a weary land; a home within the wilderness, a rest upon the way; from the burning of the noontide heat, and the burden of the day.

Upon that Cross of Jesus mine eyes at times can see; the very dying form of One who suffered there for me; and from my smitten heart with tears two wonders I confess; the wonders of redeeming love and my unworthiness.

I take, O Cross, the shadow for my abiding place; I ask no other sunshine than the sunshine of His face; content to let the world go by, to know no gain nor loss; my sinful self my only shame, my glory all the Cross."

# Summary

This book will give a clear understanding of the significance of the Cross of Christ. Those who always tell their congregations to take the Cross off of their necks or out of their properties, insisting "He is no longer on the tree. Do not put a Cross in any of your possessions."

> *"On the Cross our salvation was completed. The work of redemption of all of the people of the earth was completed, and He sacrificed Himself, once and for all, for us on the Cross."*

They will come to understand that, without the Cross, we would still be knee-deep in our sins. He shed His blood for us on the Cross. On the Cross our salvation was completed. The work of redemption of all of the people of the earth was completed, and He sacrificed Himself, once and for all, for us on the Cross.

Wearing the Cross as a ring, necklace, or bracelet, and placing any forms of it, as a symbol, in the church is a sign of rejoicing, appreciation, recognition, praises of remembrance, and joy that we are no longer sinners.

> *"It is the Cross of Christ, the Cross of sorrow, the Cross of power, the Cross of blessings, the Cross of redemption, and the Cross of reconciliation with God the Father Almighty."*

Christ washed away our sins when He was crucified on the Cross. It is the Cross of Christ, the Cross of sorrow, the Cross of power, the Cross of blessings, the Cross of redemption, and the Cross of reconciliation with God the Father Almighty.

Praises and thankfulness from earth to heaven and from heaven to earth! Christ paid it all on the Cross. We cannot take half of Christ or take what we feel comfortable with in the word of the Gospel of God.

I know a lot of churches that forbid preaching about the Cross or resurrection. They are pure false preachers of the Gospel. They are making congregations, but not converting souls into the hands of the Lord.

Apostle Paul said, "May I never boast except in the Cross of our Lord Jesus Christ, through which the world has been crucified to me, and I to the world." Gal 6:14.

## The Cross and the Crucifixion

We have to stay in the Word of God, read it, study it, expand it, and analyze it. We must ask questions if we have doubts, in order to be sure of whether we truly belong to Christ Jesus, the true Son of God, who laid His life down for us, so that we could be saved and receive eternal life.

Eternal life is for those who take the entire Gospel without throwing out any of its words, and also for those who completely surrender everything to Jesus. This means surrendering in spirit, soul, and body, as well as worshiping Him in Spirit and in truth. The Father planned, the Son carried it out, and the Holy Spirit produced.

> *"Eternal life is for those who take the entire Gospel without throwing out any of its words, and also for those who completely surrender everything to Jesus."*

The Cross of Christ was the Father's plan from the beginning of creation in the Garden of Eden. The Cross of Christ is the Father's blessing to the people of the world because that is where God sacrificed His one and only begotten Son to the world, so that those who believed in Him would not perish but would have eternal life.

The Lord Jesus Christ reconciled us with God when He willingly and perfectly fulfilled the law with the Spirit of obedience and totally surrendered to the will of God the Father. He became flesh and dwelled among us. We behold His glory, the glory of the only begotten Son of the Father.

He became the Lamb of God that took away the sins of the world. He is the second Adam, in all creation and in the covenant of grace that God the Father planned with Him.

> *"Reconciliation through the blood of Jesus Christ covers our sins. Our sins will not appear in God's sight. God no longer remembers our sins."*

Christ is the head of the Church, as well as the head of mankind, throughout creation. Christ is the mediator of a new covenant. The old things have passed away; behold, all things become new! (2 Cor 5:17) With His divine power, Christ has united himself with His creations and He is ready to take them to heaven.

Christ's shedding of His own blood for the remission of our sins through suffering revealed His holiness and His infinite power. Reconciliation through the blood of Jesus Christ covers our sins. Our sins will not appear in God's sight. God no longer remembers our sins. Atonement for sin has been made; we have peace with God. Hallelujah!

# Final Word

The Cross of Jesus Christ is:

The Cross of love
The Cross of mercy, the Cross of joy
The Cross of great compassion
The Cross of power
The Cross of peace
The Cross of promise
The Cross of fulfillment
The Cross of goodness of God
The Cross of knowledge
The Cross of kindness
The Cross of humbleness
The Cross of justification
The Cross of wisdom
The Cross of communion
The Cross of surrender

The Cross of sanctification
The Cross of justification
The Cross of magnification
The Cross of salvation
The Cross of sinners and the lost
The Cross of message to the world
The Cross of the new earth
The Cross of glory
The Cross of worship
The Cross of truth
The Cross of life
The Cross of forgiveness
The Cross of righteousness
The Cross of adoration
The Cross of grace
The Cross of light
The Cross of blessings
The Cross of faithfulness
The Cross of perfect obedience
The Cross of suffering
The Cross of new covenant
The Cross of message of peace to the world

## The Cross and the Crucifixion

It is the one and only Cross where the Son of God was crucified.

Near the Cross of Jesus, His mother was there at the foot of the Cross. We have to see the Lamb as the light of heaven. The Lamb is the lamp. "The city does not need the sun or the moon to shine on it, for the glory of God gives it light, and the Lamb is its lamp." Rev 21:23.

Light is the sign of joy of the saints. Peace on earth and good will to men. On the Cross is where our salvation is completed.

# Benediction

May the blood of Jesus Christ, the true Son of man and the true Son of God, that was shed on the Cross for the remission of the sins of all people in the whole world flow into our very blood and cleanse all our sins, purifying and making us alive and one in Him, as He and the Father are one.

In the mighty Holy name of Jesus Christ I pray, a name above all names. Jesus Christ, our Redeemer King, accepts our prayer, Amen.

May the grace of our Lord Jesus Christ, the Love of God, and the communion of the Holy Spirit, be with us now and forever more. Amen.

# Biblical Index

Genesis 3:23, 6:8, 1:27, 49:24, 3:15, 2:8
Exodus 12:22
Deuteronomy 21:23
Psalms 69:21, 22:31, 139:1-4, 40:7-8
Ecclesiastes 12:7
Isaiah 53:6
Zechariah 12:1
Malachi 4:2
Matthew 18:21-22, 27:42, 20:28, 1:21
Mark 15:24, 17:22, 10:45, 15:39
Luke 22:42, 12:50, 23:46, 23:34, 46, 10:30, 2:34-35, 2:49, 23:43
John 19:26, 25, 28, 10:18, 4:7, 19:29, 10:29, 15:13, 10:30, 2:34-35, 2:49, 4:14, 6:35, 14:26,19:30, 17:4, 6:35, 40, 10:28-29,19:26-27, 19:28-30, 1:29, 17:2, 12, 4:10, 7:37-38, 4:34, 17:4, 15, 16, 17
Roman 6:4, 6:10, 8:10, 8:1, 3:24, 5:9, 1:16, 6:11, 5:17-18
1st Corinthians 3:11, 2:2, 1:30, 2:9, 1:18, 1:23-24
2nd Corinthians 2:15-17, 5:19, 12:4
Galatians 6:14, 3:13-14, 2:20, 6:14

## The Cross and the Crucifixion

Ephesians 5:2, 1:7
Philippians 3:18, 4:19
Titus 3:5
Hebrews 10:12, 7:25
1st Peter 3:18, 1:5, 2:21-23
1st John 3:2, 3:1
Revelation 2:23

Books previously published by the author Grace Dola Balogun by Grace Religious Books Publishing & Distributors, Inc.

**PRAYER THE SOURCE OF STRENGTH FOR LIFE** – English Edition

*Prayer the Source of Strength for Life* is a powerful book that will energize your spirit to pray more and more until the prayer is part of your life and until the gate of heaven is opened and your prayer is answered. Your prayer life will change your life.

**LA ORACION FUENTE DE FORTALEZA PARA LA VIDA – Spanish Edition.**

Dios nos dio el poder de la oracion, quiere que lo usemos; debemos illamar, comunicarnos con el en todo lo que estemos pasando. El espera saber de nosotros.

# THE SPIRIT POWER VOLUME I & II

These two books discuss the power of the Holy Spirit in the life of believers of Jesus Christ.

The Power of the Spirit of God begins from the creation of the world up until today. That power will also continue until Christ return to reign.

# About the Author

Grace Dola Balogun graduated from Fordham University Graduate School of Religion and Religious Education in the year 2010 with an M.A. in Religion and Religious Education. She has been a prayer mentor and advisor for many Christians of all denominations since 1988.

Visit her online at:
gracereligiousbookspublishers.com
Prayerstrengthforlife.com
Spiritpower.info
salvationcompleted.com
Facebook
GSTwitter@prayersource

# To Order This Book

To order additional copies of this book,
please E-mail:
info@gracereligiousbookspublishers.com

This book may also be ordered from 30,000 wholesalers, retailers, and booksellers in the U. S., and in Canada and over 100 countries globally.

To contact Grace Dola Balogun for an interview or a speaking engagement, please E-mail:
info@gracereligiousbookspublishers.com

The Spirit and the bride say, "Come!"
And let the one who hears say, "Come!"
Let the one who is thirsty come;
and let the one who wishes take
the free gift of the water of life.

Revelation 22:17

*MARANATHA!*

*COME, LORD JESUS!*

www.ingramcontent.com/pod-product-compliance
Lightning Source LLC
Chambersburg PA
CBHW072336300426
44109CB00042B/1634